MY DIFFERENTLY TUNED-IN CHILD

The Right Place for Strength-Based Solutions

Teresa Currivan, LMFT

My Differently Tuned-In Child
Copyright © 2020 by Teresa Currivan, LMFT

All rights reserved under the International and Pan-American Copyright Conventions. No part of this book may be reproduced or transmitted in any form or by any means, electronic or mechanical, including photocopying, recording, or by any information storage and retrieval system, without permission in writing from the publisher.

Warning: the unauthorized reproduction or distribution of this copyrighted work is illegal. Criminal copyright infringement, including infringement without monetary gain, is investigated by the FBI and is punishable by up to 5 years in prison and a fine of $250,000.

Print ISBN: 978-0-578-72354-9
Edited by: Miriam Schaffer
Interior formatting and cover art by: Rising Sign Books

Published by: Right Place Publishing

THE RIGHT PLACE LEARNING and THE RIGHT PLACE LEARNING CENTER are registered trademarks of Teresa Currivan

This book is dedicated to my mom, with love.

Introduction

My Story, Your Story, and the Answers

This book is a collection of articles I have written over the years. I decided to compile them into one volume so that parents would have the information and knowledge I've gained over my years helping families, as well as from my experience parenting a differently tuned-in child.

When my son was 5 years old, he was having difficulty in school both socially and academically. Like many parents, I became frustrated trying to figure out how to navigate the world of professionals and educators, many of whom had a piece of the puzzle of my son but couldn't help me put them all together. I was eventually able to figure out how to get to the bottom of things so that my son could be seen for the truly amazing person he is, and not only as a label or pathology. The result has been that, today, as a teenager, he is finding his way. During that time, I wished I had a place to go — and someone who could oversee all that I needed to figure out, more quickly and less expensively – I wished I'd had the right place.

Today, I support parents while we figure out the best way to help their child and their family. Over the years, I have learned that each differently tuned-in child comes with strengths and challenges in unique combinations. I developed the Currivan Protocol™ out of this experience. It is a comprehensive assessment and treatment plan that involves identifying what can be treated, accepting challenges, and identifying and embracing strengths. I was driven to create it out of my desire to help struggling children quickly, effectively and less expensively than what I had experienced.

I created The Right Place Learning Center so that parents with differently tuned-in children can finally get the unique help they need — from visual-spatial tutors, to parent support groups, to private coaching and relationship help specifically designed for your specific challenges — so that you can take a deep breath and know you are in the right place.

By reading the advice and insights in this book, I hope that parents do not have to struggle as I did but will begin to gain a clearer understanding of their child and his or her behavior.

I understand that parents and teachers are given many challenges in this fast-paced world. My intention in shedding light on the issues faced by differently tuned-in children and their parents is to make everyone's life less stressful. I hope that you can find the path you need to help your child and yourself, especially if you have been previously misunderstood.

You will see various words in this book to mean differently tuned-in. Differently tuned-in, differently wired, and exceptional can mean any non-neurotypical learner such as a child with dyslexia, ADHD or who is on the autism spectrum. Gifted means high IQ, and twice-exceptional means gifted with one or more learning or emotional challenges.

While I hope you will read this book from beginning to end, you may also choose to read those chapters that call out to you and your particular situation. Many of the chapters share stories of children whose names have been changed for their privacy. You may find your child in their stories. I hope you will learn from them, quickly get to the root of the issues you're facing, and watch as your child gains self-esteem and thrives with friends, family, and what may feel like a newfound freedom to be themselves.

TABLE OF CONTENTS

Introduction i

How I Struggled in School as a Visual-Spatial Learner... 1

Gifted in the School Setting 11

The Other Side of Being Gifted 22

The Visual-Spatial Learner.............................. 26

How to Facilitate Your Visual-Spatial Learner at Home 35

Making Sense of Your Gifted Child's Diagnosis: A Review of *Misdiagnosis and Dual Diagnosis of Gifted Children* and Adults 41

The School Meeting... 49

Developmental Milestones of Executive Functioning in Differently Tuned-In Kids 53

Specific Challenges of Understanding Gifted Boys 56

6 Signs Your Preschooler May Be Gifted and Why It's Important to Know 62

How to Obtain Proper Testing for the Exceptional Learner... 72

How Can I Tell Sensory Issues From Other Issues? 76

Why is High-Achieving Synonymous with Being Gifted? Because We Didn't Listen to This Woman 82

Unschooling the Differently Wired 88

How to Deschool an Exceptional Learner 95

Why Intrinsic Motivation is Essential to Educating Our Exceptional Learners 106

The Benefits of Free Play in Nature 114

5 Traits of the Young Empath 118

Empathy Always Wins 120

Open Letter to a "Gifted" Teen 124

Boredom in Motherhood: the Good, the Bad, and the Ugly 127

Bibliography 131

About the Author 133

HOW I STRUGGLED IN SCHOOL AS A VISUAL-SPATIAL LEARNER

After having my own child, and as I helped him and other children find their learning styles, I learned that my style of thinking and learning had a name: visual-spatial. I was elated to know that I wasn't alone in my ability to think in images and then translate into language. What I was finding out, however, was that many of these visual-spatial learners are acting out, or becoming bored, sometimes even being labeled as defiant, or having other challenges in school. Perhaps a visual-spatial child's defiance is a way of saying, "Couldn't we make this more interesting?"

Visual-spatial thinkers and learners see things in pictures and feel them in spaces before converting them to language.

Experts today say that they are gifted — a word that made me cringe until I understood its full meaning. This is how I describe visual-spatial learners:

Visual-spatial learners take in, create, and process ideas in a very different way than auditory-sequential learners. They think and process in pictures and spatially rather than words. If you can imagine a "pre-verbal" thought - that brief millisecond before your thought becomes words, you may be able to understand this. They are coming up with new ideas while listening to descriptions in the same thought process. Therefore giving auditory instructions that have many steps to a visual-spatial person may not bring success. At the same time, these thinkers may be able to solve seemingly complex tasks that others are not able to. They tend to think holistically, connecting all of the bigger picture issues and may sometimes miss details. (Although they can also get hyper-focused on details in many cases.) They can seem to have executive functioning challenges because they do their best thinking when in a flow state, which can be contrary to keeping track of time and being organized. These challenges can be managed when understood. They are often gifted in the areas of math, emotions, technology, and the arts.

In our schools, most teaching techniques are designed for linear-sequential learners whose learning progresses in a step-by-step manner from easy to difficult material. Subjects are taught in a step-by-step fashion, practiced with drill and repetition, assessed under timed conditions, and then reviewed. It approaches problem-solving and learning in a systematic manner, using a series of logical steps:

- Memorize the math facts and then do algebra.
- Learn to read and write and then make up a story or "write."

This is the counterpart to the visual-spatial style. By adulthood, we typically use both of these styles to a certain extent. But more and more, I see children who are further on the visual-spatial spectrum who don't yet have the more sequential learning skills that are required in school at an early age, (and who often develop them later than a typical child).

Since our education system does not, for the most part, support visual-spatial learners, we have many children who are not equipped for success in our schools.

Some cultures are dominantly visual-spatial. In my experience, it seems that families from some non-dominant cultures within the United States tend to be more open to understanding visual-spatial thinking. For many of us, it can be difficult to see that the norm in the U.S. and in our education system is the linear-sequential thinking style because we are immersed in it. And most visual-spatial thinkers, I'm guessing, like me, don't know it has a name, or even that some people have a different way of thinking.

I hope my story helps to more precisely illustrate the visual-spatial learning style.

In third grade, I remember my older sister helping me memorize math facts with flashcards over and over. I looked up to my sister and enjoyed her attention. I would have let her test me with flashcards forever, if just to spend time together. Like me, many of these kids are relational learners — it's all about who they are learning with! Above all, **I wanted to get it.** But many of the math facts did not stick. Before third grade, I had lively, creative teachers, but that year I had, through my young eyes, a boring, crotchety teacher who focused only on facts. I remember sitting bored and spaced out in class, and it was as though the lights went dim and everything turned grey. I believe that this was the pivotal moment when a light went out in me. I no longer brought my curiosity to school, and perhaps unconsciously, knew that school was not where **life** happened. School was all about memorization; I would buckle down and get by. But in the process, I became disconnected from a part of myself, from my heart and my own intelligence. From that point forward, I learned test-taking skills that would allow me to memorize facts, but not connect them to meaning. I would forget them in a week.

In high school, I remember trying to memorize the symbolism of Shakespeare for a test. Rose equals love. I memorized it and checked that box on the test. I got by with mostly Cs.

However, I remember enjoying high school history. I loved the stories and the way my teachers told them. But the tests were painful. One of the test questions I studied for was "List the causes of WW II." When my own son was having problems in school and had to be homeschooled in second grade, he asked me what caused WW II. We researched it. He watched documentaries, listened to historical fiction, enacted battle scenes, and found many answers to his question. At first, if you were to ask him, he could probably tell you a story about some causes and perhaps a not-so-helpful treaty from WW I. The more he learns, however, the more complicated he understands the answer to be. Recently, a few years after his initial question, he became obsessed with reenacting Dunkirk at the beach with friends. This was his way of synthesizing his knowledge of WW II, as well as processing the movie. I need only to go along for the ride with him to know that he is learning. Over time. No quiz necessary. I continue to find educational methods and teachers who understand his learning style, where he can study in depth what is engaging to him, even if the topics are beyond his grade level.

In college, I read the science fiction novel, *The Making of the Representative for Planet 8*, by Doris Lessing. While reading it, I remember feeling sadness about my mom who had died a few years earlier. I can't remember what I wrote in my essay, but I remember flat, snowy plains, and having feelings of loss. When I received my essay back, it was filled with red ink. The teacher wrote that I was wrong; the novel was about the extinction of a race. It is interesting that because Lessing is such a descriptively rich writer, I had somehow absorbed a deeper meaning of the novel and felt it, but was not able to process it into my intellect. Did my teacher think that I hadn't read the book? That I was incapable? That I didn't care? Or that I was not very intelligent? I'll never know.

> *What we now know about visual-spatial learners is that we need more time to translate our images (visual-spatial) into words (which are linear).*

In my case, since I had essentially been cut off from my natural way of learning, I needed help knowing that my images and feelings mattered and, in fact, were my way of knowing and experiencing the world.

Today, I see many students trying to cope with an education system that doesn't fit their learning style. Unfortunately, many professionals in education and psychology who are trying to help these children are trained to focus on behavior rather than learning style, and these children are often given labels that only partly address their problem, or that do not address their problem at all.

I think we can all agree that when a child is having difficulties it's best to get to the truth of the problem, seek resolution and support the child at the earliest possible age.

One highly visual-spatial third grader was refusing to go to school and daily cutting herself on the arm. Her parents were told by a mental health professional that their daughter may have ADHD and depression. Medication was suggested. Instead, the parents decided to pull the child from school. The child stopped cutting immediately and was exhibiting happy behavior. This was only the beginning of their journey in discovering what their child needed, but these parents took a risk and trusted their own knowledge of their child.

Schools designed for visual-spatial learners are going to be the most successful fit for these children. Based on a homeschooling model, these are micro-schools that follow the intellectual curiosity of the children and are project-based and learner-driven.

They are able to address the varying needs that children have by using techniques such as Montessori math, a process-oriented, tactile and visual way of learning math. They will also use technology and experiential learning methods that relate to real-world use. Their high student-teacher ratio and high teacher retention are key to creating and maintaining important relationships that develop over the years. These schools also benefit linear-spatial learners by helping them to access their creativity and problem-solving skills, as well as applying their skills for practical use.

My Differently Tuned-In Child

I hope our public school system can learn from the techniques with which these micro-schools and homeschoolers are finding success. It goes without saying that many parents cannot afford to homeschool or pay for a private school. I think I speak for many parents who have discovered a successful educational fit for their child, that there is great concern in our school systems' ability to educate every child well.

I recently spotted a student being observed by one of his teachers. She was looking at him with a knowing gaze, that, without any words communicated how she **saw** him: she understood how complex his thinking was. He was working hard to communicate it, and she respected him. How amazing would it have been for me to have been given recognition from a teacher as a child? To smell a rose as a way of understanding what Shakespeare was referring to, to be trusted enough to explore what I thought it meant for me, and what it meant in the context of his play? What if I had been able to know that my own agency and intellect had a role to play in figuring it all out? And, more importantly, what if I had had this all reflected back from my teachers that I was getting it, that learning was fun, and that my experiences and thoughts mattered?

How many more children today could be benefiting from a teacher's knowing gaze? How much more joy could come to both teacher and student if the former were given the opportunities and resources to really know her students and be able to honestly say, with or without words, "I see you, your intellect, your heart, and I admire what you are doing."?

How amazing it would be for all learners to be allowed to experience education in this way.

Gifted in the School Setting

For many of us, the word "gifted" brings to mind very specific assumptions. It's an elite label that we put on high-achieving children for whom things will come easily. We believe that success is pretty much guaranteed.

But, not necessarily.

Many parents who seek my help have been told that their child is gifted. They've breathed a sigh of relief knowing that "he'll figure it out, he's smart." At the same time, they may have received the news that their child has a learning challenge such as dyslexia, or has an emotional problem. How can this be? Aren't these contradictions? Too often, I find that the connection between these two is not made. This can cause confusion about the child's ability to learn as well as their mental health.

> *Giftedness means having a brain that is wired differently. While no two gifted people are the same, gifted individuals can have extreme sensitivities, intensities, creative and intellectual drives and perfectionism. The inner world of the gifted child can be much larger than he knows how to express and sometimes learning how to be in the world can be difficult.*

While many people associate the term "special needs" with children who have developmental or learning challenges, it means only that a child has "special needs." Gifted children are also a special needs population.

The Columbus Group, a small group of individuals (parents, educators, and psychologists) who, in the late 1980s worked with highly to profoundly gifted children in Columbus, Ohio, sought to redefine giftedness in terms of the inner experience of the individual. They define giftedness as follows:

"Giftedness is *asynchronous development* in which advanced cognitive abilities and heightened intensity combine to create inner experiences and awareness that are qualitatively different from the norm. This asynchrony increases with higher intellectual capacity. The uniqueness of the gifted renders them particularly vulnerable and requires modifications in parenting, teaching and counseling in order for them to develop optimally." (The Columbus Group, 1991).

Asynchronous development means that the child is not following the developmental milestones that we expect from a typical child. He may say his first word at four months, but not read until age 10. She may hold a calculus book in one hand and a teddy bear in the other at age 9.

Before she even entered school, Clara (name has been changed) was a science enthusiast and loved horses and all animals. When her mother attended her first parent-teacher meeting, the kindergarten teacher reported that she enjoyed the level at which Clara could communicate about most topics. Further, she loved Clara's participation in all class discussions. When a guest science expert came to class, he was taken aback by her higher level and in-depth knowledge on various science topics. However, the teacher also said, "The other children don't like your daughter." Clara despised coloring, worksheets and any "busy" work that was assigned to her. She responded to these by ripping the pages with her crayon out of frustration. She told her mom, "It's just what the teachers give us when they have other work to do."

By second grade, Clara was having a harder time with the many worksheets and homework. During a math homework session with her dad, she yelled out of frustration, "If I already did the problem, why do I have to keep doing all of these!" referring to the many pages of math problems. Meanwhile, her mother was becoming aware that Clara was being left out and bullied by other children on the schoolyard. When Clara's mom discussed this with the school principal, she was met with defensiveness, and events were often blamed on Clara. Clara's mother took some time off from work and helped out in the classroom in order to observe and better understand what was going on. She noticed that Clara had become very quiet during class discussions. The second-grade teacher didn't know that Clara had previously been an engaged, articulate student. Clara's mother felt her daughter was a stream of contradictions.

Clara was slower to read and to do math than her peers. After some testing, it was decided that she would be pulled out of class for special education tutoring. (She was tested as "gifted" for verbal vocabulary, but very low in other areas.) Clara's mother didn't quite know why, but she knew that this tutoring would not work well for Clara. However, she wasn't sure how else to help her. Clara often complained about the "baby" books she was assigned to read at school. Once when Clara's mother happened to be watching Clara's first-grade teacher testing Clara's comprehension skills, there was a misunderstanding about whether water ran "over," or "under," the ground. The teacher thought Clara didn't understand the words "under," and "over," and said, "No, water runs *over* the ground," pointing to the very simple book with a picture of a river. Her mother tried to explain that Clara was probably referring to aquifers, which run under the ground. She didn't want to be seen as uncooperative, so she didn't press the issue. Sure enough, the first few weeks of her special education tutoring, Clara was in trouble for running down the halls, away from her remedial tutoring sessions.

At this point, the school psychologist was suggesting that Clara was "defiant" and was going to reevaluate her. Clara's mother was starting to worry that Clara was defiant; that there was something wrong with her child. Even her behavior after school was becoming more difficult to manage. Clara would have meltdowns that would last until bedtime. The Clara that used to be, the sweet, curious, engaged, loving, spontaneous, and joyful girl was disappearing before her eyes. Clara wasn't even drawing pictures of horses as much as she used to. Sometimes on the weekends she would return to her old self, if the family spent a day in nature with a lot of physical activity and quiet time, or if she spent time with non-school friends, or if horses and other animals were involved. But she felt that Clara's spark was slowly fading. She wasn't sure if this was part of the normal struggles of growing up and fitting in, or something was going very wrong. She feared it was the latter, but didn't know what to do. This is when a friend suggested that Clara might be gifted. Clara's mother thought this was a joke because Clara was having problems in school. (Her high vocabulary didn't seem relevant to what was happening.) But when she sought my help, read about giftedness, and talked with other mothers who had gifted children, she was shocked to discover the similarities in their stories.

Even though Clara had been tested through the school system, I suggested that she be tested through a center that does in-depth, individual assessments with a qualitative component. Clara was assessed to be in the exceptionally gifted category. Clara's mother was given very specific information, such as the fact that Clara is an introvert, (a surprise to her mother), and that she was a highly visual-spatial thinker. The report included information about Clara's sensitivities, propensity for ADHD and sensory issues. While this isn't the case for every gifted child, since Clara was highly gifted, she would need special classes designed for gifted children that offer more depth, density, and opportunities for her to use her imagination while learning.

Clara's mother discovered that the reason the math worksheets didn't work for Clara was that she had already integrated the knowledge, and repeating the "same thing over and over" was more than just tedious.

In the words of Linda Silverman, another expert on gifted visual-spatial learners, doing repetitive work, "… is like being asked to remove the egg out of the cake batter once you've mixed it in." Most gifted learners integrate knowledge as they learn and need to learn and to be tested on a higher level. The more gifted a child is, the more asynchronous she can be, and the more she will require early identification and support.

While homeschooling is an excellent option for highly to profoundly gifted students, with my help, Clara's mother found a school that is a good fit. The teachers have a deep understanding of how creative children learn and are able to offer ways of learning that cater to her need for creativity and higher, in-depth learning that most highly to profoundly gifted children need. The school values social-emotional learning as a top priority, and Clara has been able to process her high perfectionism, high sensitivities, and strong will. The school staff sees many children who have not had great experiences with authority figures. Rather than label them as "defiant," they help the students through this while recognizing that a strong will is a common gifted trait. (As you search for schools for your child, please keep in mind that, ironically, many "gifted" schools will not work for learners who are in the highly to profoundly gifted ranges. Some cater to an older definition of giftedness, which usually translates to more stringent rules, and perhaps even more tedious work than the norm, which can backfire.)

While Clara continued not to read, the school allowed her to dictate stories and to listen to books. This kept her engaged in storytelling while she found her own way. Her reading was supported in other ways that she enjoyed, such as a spelling game app and having to check her own dictation. A year and a half later, she was able to read high-school-level novels.

What Clara's mother found interesting was how sensitive Clara was. As is more typical in boys, she often hid her sensitivities under anger or tantrums. Clara seemed to be going in both directions — both shutting down during class and running away and ripping up papers. With my help, Clara's mother was able to side coach her about her strong will and her constant fight with authority figures in a way that acknowledged the need to disagree, but in a healthy way. This, of course, is a process, but good for Clara to experience before her teen years.

Clara is now in sixth grade and her mother reports that she is doing well. She is back to her talkative, intense, sensitive, and engaged self. Most importantly, she has good friends with whom she can relate, some she met in school, and some from gifted groups outside of school. Her mother feels like she has her daughter back. While it took some time, and her parents continue to need support from time to time, they feel they are better equipped to raise Clara and better able to hold boundaries as they help her navigate her intensities, sensitivities, and intense drive to experience and learn. Her mother understands Clara's deep need for downtime and sees how important it is to allow her to process her ideas in her unusual, creative ways. Her father knows that running and playing "gymnastics stunts" is not only fun for his child, but it is essential. As her mother has discovered, their entire family is gifted on some level, and she has sought my help in understanding their family dynamics as well as her own struggles as a gifted mother. Their knowledge of Clara's differences and how to help her through difficult times is what I hope for every gifted child. What I strongly advocate is even earlier intervention when possible.

Why is it so difficult to identify and get help for the gifted child? By the time my own child was having difficulties in school, I had already received my master's in counseling psychology and was a licensed Marriage and Family Therapist. Not once did giftedness enter into my education or training even though giftedness can influence a diagnosis. This is the case for most psychologists, therapists, and teachers, including school psychologists. In retrospect, in my work in community mental health with children and families, I suspect that some of the children I worked with were gifted. Clearly, there needs to be more awareness of giftedness in the fields of psychology and education. My hope is that as schools adopt child-centered approaches, these needs will be met.

If you have a gifted child, or suspect that your child is gifted, because he or she seems to be struggling, I recommend obtaining gifted support. Your understanding of your child will become deeper and clearer and your child's understanding of himself can help guide him into adulthood.

The Other Side of Being Gifted

For most of us, the word "gifted" conjures images of privilege and automatic success. But what if I told you that gifted people also suffer because of this false notion?

WHAT IS GIFTEDNESS?

Gifted people reside in every culture, every race, every country on this planet. What most can agree on is that giftedness means a higher IQ. While this is usually true, what is less commonly known is that it can also involve acute sensitivities to noises, smells, and other environmental stimulation, an unusually strong sense of justice, high creativity, and sometimes crippling perfectionism. The personality "quirks" that manifest from these characteristics are often misunderstood by not only lay people, but by educators and other professionals, including those in mental health. This lack of understanding impacts not only the gifted individuals and their family members but all of us.

In the book, *Misdiagnosis and Dual Diagnosis of Gifted Children*, Webb, et al. explain that the gifted individual's inherent drives "together result in an intense idealism and concern with social and moral issues, which can create anxiety, depression, and a sharp challenging of others who do not share their concerns."

WHAT HAPPENS WHEN WE MISUNDERSTAND OR IGNORE GIFTEDNESS?

The most common problem I work with is the child who is struggling in school because he doesn't think or learn at the same level or same way as the rest of the classroom.

Many gifted learners I work with are what are called visual-spatial learners (those who learn holistically). They, like all children, desperately want to fit in. But in our typical classrooms designed for linear-sequential learners (those who learn step-by-step and in succession), they cannot. These are kids who are highly creative at math, art, tech, science, or emotions in ways that are often different than the "norm." As many schools become more focused on linear-sequential teaching and testing, these children have fewer learning tools at their disposal. As a result, they may act out, become silent and depressed, and, because they have different learning needs, are often diagnosed with learning problems (rather than giftedness). In fact, gifted kids are more likely than any other population to be misdiagnosed. While their needs would be best met through more, faster, and different, they may be put in special ed where the pace is slower and memorization is often emphasized. This exacerbates their boredom and can lead to depression, higher incidence of ADHD symptoms, acting out, and deep self-esteem, and social issues. The result: we have a recipe for disaster and suffering for both the gifted child and for other students in their classroom. Years later, the impact remains as many gifted adults today ironically don't view themselves as smart, and are underusing their strengths. Not good for our society as a whole.

What I've observed is that we get stuck in trying to understand this in terms of our "normal" selves and "normal" people. Gifted individuals are wired differently, and I believe that if we were to truly understand giftedness, with all of its challenges and actual gifts, we would also be able to appreciate ourselves more – no matter where on the scale we fall.

If your child is struggling and you think he or she may be highly gifted, please seek help from someone who understands their unique way of being in the world. Forcing them to fit into a "round hole" can be harmful. When allowed to learn as they need to, and socialize with those they naturally connect with, they will find their place among the rest of us, so we can all benefit.

The Visual-Spatial Learner

John, as his mother will explain in an exhausted tone, is an energetic child. He loves Legos, creating unique contraptions, and appreciates complex conceptual challenges. But in kindergarten and first grade, he struggled with many subjects. While he enjoyed discussing larger math concepts like infinity and fractals, he battled with basic math facts, spelling, and even writing (and was later diagnosed with dyslexia).

John is also very sensitive. When he knew that his teachers or other children were frustrated with him, he, in turn, acted out in frustration. He was eventually asked to leave first grade due to behavior problems.

In one interaction with John, then seven years old, he informed me that "the parts of a tree are all the same." I had a feeling he was onto something, so I encouraged him: "But an apple isn't the same as its bark or its leaves. I can't eat the bark of an apple tree, but I can eat the apple," I said.

"Yes," he said, searching for words to describe a concept that seemed so clear in his mind. "But the leaves, the apple, the bark, the wood, the roots – it's all the same, *through and through*." When I asked how he knew this, he strained to articulate his idea. Eventually, though he wasn't able to give me the proper term, I believe he was describing what we call DNA.

John is a visual-spatial learner.

These children think in pictures and pre-verbal thoughts rather than in words. They have a different brain organization than auditory-sequential learners. They learn better visually and need to make a connection between things, rather than given directions auditorily and in a specific order.

Additionally, visual-spatial learners tend to learn holistically. This results in their sometimes arriving at solutions without going through the usual steps. Showing your work, often required by teachers, may be impossible and sometimes results in suspicion of cheating. Visual-spatial learners may succeed in solving difficult problems while finding simpler tasks a challenge. Teachers might interpret this kind of student as being obstinate or contrary.

Most teaching techniques in our schools are designed for linear-sequential learners whose learning progresses from easy to difficult material. Subjects are taught in a step-by-step fashion, practiced with drill and repetition, assessed under timed conditions, and then reviewed. Problem solving and learning is done in a systematic manner, using a series of logical steps: Memorize the math facts and then do algebra, or learn to read and write, and then write your own story.

While these techniques work for some learners, they are counter to the visual-spatial style. More and more, I see children on the visual-spatial spectrum who don't yet have the sequential learning skills required early on in school.

HOW TO RECOGNIZE A VISUAL-SPATIAL LEARNER

Below are some traits of visual-spatial learners as devised by Linda Silverman, PhD. The appearance of one, or even several of these, does not necessarily indicate a visual-spatial learner. But if many indicators are evident, it's worth looking into:
- Thinks in images instead of words
- Resists demonstrating what she or he knows

- Has trouble with timed tests
- Takes things apart to find out how they work
- Is frustrated with writing assignments
- Solves problems in unusual ways
- Doesn't memorize math facts easily
- Reaches correct conclusions without apparent steps
- Dislikes public speaking
- Is not a good speller
- Doesn't budget time well
- Doesn't have neat handwriting
- Is extraordinarily imaginative
- Oral expression is much better than written expression
- Is not well organized

(from *Upside-Down Brilliance: The Visual-Spatial Learner, 2002,* Kreger Silverman)

One thing I would add to this list is the spatial component of thought. It is as though thoughts come in "chunks," or "globs," or preverbal thoughts. Complex ideas present in preverbal units, and it's in this way that many visual-spatial thinkers synthesize thoughts. So, I would add, "thinks in preverbal chunks." So much about being visual-spatial gets lost in translation when trying to put the visual-spatial thought into words (which are linear).

Today, I see many students trying to cope with an education system that doesn't fit their learning style. Unfortunately, most professionals tasked with helping these children are trained to, (or only have time to), focus on behavior rather than learning style. As a result, these children are often given labels that only partly address their problem, or that don't address their problem at all.

WHAT CAN WE DO?

- Homeschooling, or attending schools designed for visual-spatial learners, is the best way to educate these children when possible. Following the intellectual curiosity of the child with project-based and learner-driven techniques is helpful. Addressing the varying needs of children through techniques such as Montessori math, (a process-oriented, tactile, and visual way of learning math), technology, and experiential learning methods are also helpful. Additionally, having a high student-teacher ratio and high teacher retention is key to creating and maintaining important relationships that develop over the years, as visual-spatial children are relational learners.

- For families who are unable to homeschool, or attend a private school, understanding how your child thinks and learns will be helpful. Using this information to parent and communicate with his teacher is going to be important. One simple change that can make a huge positive impact for many of these students is finding alternatives to traditional homework and quizzes. (For those lucky enough to have one-on-one tutoring, the same applies and can be ideal.) Keep all after school and home activities child-led as much as possible. Seek help from a professional who is knowledgeable about visual-spatial children if there are behavior issues. More often than not, the behaviors can be due to the child's misinterpretation that they are not good enough when really the issue is an educational mismatch. Even when you can't fix their education, you can side coach them at home with your deeper understanding of what is really going on. How you interpret the situation is more important than getting them the right school. Seek help for yourself in getting clarity so that you can guide your child when needed.

- Additionally, allowing your child to explore and learn outside of school in a way that suits them is going to be important. Is she obsessed with YouTube videos about something educational like science experiments, or even Spongebob? Embrace it. Does he need to download all that he has learned by talking to you, another adult, or a peer who has similar interests? Does she want to learn about stop motion animation, but doesn't want to take a class? Does he want to continue with dramatic play, even though his same-aged friends are done with that? I'd say go with all of this whenever possible. This is your child's way of learning and integrating knowledge.

- Find your child like-minded friends (yes, they are out there!) Organize a monthly get together for chess, Harry Potter, Dungeons and Dragons, or whatever your child is excited about. Do the work to stay connected to that one friend he hit it off with about supernovas back in first grade.

A SUCCESS STORY

Jeannie, a highly visual-spatial first grader, was refusing to go to school and cutting her arm daily. A mental health professional told her parents that she may have ADHD and depression.

Her parents decided to pull Jeannie from school. She stopped cutting immediately and exhibited happy behavior. This marked the beginning of the family's journey in discovering Jeannie's needs. They've since sought my help, and as part of that, obtained appropriate assessments. When seeking help for your child, find someone who you feel "gets" them: their quirkiness, their intelligence, and the depth of their emotions. Remember to trust your instincts on this one.

Jeannie tested as being highly creative, highly sensitive, highly visual-spatial, and highly gifted. She now shows no signs of depression. Here is what we found helpful for Jeannie.

The first year Jeannie's mother homeschooled her, using a child-led approach. Jeannie was allowed to read the Harry Potter books as much as she wanted, (an obsession of Jeannie's, as she wore her Harry Potter robe everywhere). As part of her schooling, her mother found a homeschool class where Jeannie and other children explored the stories in depth by creating art, enacting scenes, and even choosing a character to be all day. All of this allowed Jeannie to process in depth what she loved about the books, and what she was yearning to learn more deeply. In this class, Jeannie met friends with mutual interests (and mutual learning styles), and processed some of the rich information about being human that these amazing books have to offer, addressing social skills along the way (without calling it "Social Skills").

The second year, Jeannie attended a micro-school designed specifically for highly gifted, visual-spatial learners. Her teachers allowed her to study in depth what engaged her, even if topics were beyond her grade level.

Now, Jeannie continues to be engaged, and while she previously had difficulties connecting with others, she has a close group of friends with shared interests. She even reaches out to those who do not share her interests. Jeannie, now in fifth grade, continues to thrive at her current school. Her parents continue to embrace her different learning style at home.

It is my hope that our public school system can learn from techniques with which homeschoolers and certain micro-schools are finding success and incorporate them into their methodologies. Visual-spatial children are key to our societal advancement. As Silverman has found, they are often some of the most gifted creatively, technologically, mathematically, and emotionally.

Visual-spatial children are an integral part of what our future needs to be.

How to Facilitate Your Visual-Spatial Learner at Home

If your visual-spatial (VS) child is at a more typical school that emphasizes traditional learning methods, please know that there is plenty you can do to facilitate their learning at home. These kids never stop learning, and often do their more important work after school and on the weekends (and yes, sometimes at midnight). Here are eight things you can do to facilitate their learning.

1. SUPPORT THEIR PROJECTS AND CURIOSITIES

This is the easiest and clearest thing you can do. Help them find the tools, the classes, the glue, the shows, the entrepreneurial endeavors. Exhausted? See if you can get a neighbor kid to help, even a mentor if you can. High school students are often a good fit to mentor younger students. (Many VS high schoolers thrive when given real responsibilities, such as teaching a younger child, especially for pay.)

2. ALLOW FOR PLENTY OF UNSTRUCTURED TIME

If they are at a school that is very structured, they may need plenty of unstructured time at home. Some kids will need downtime after school before they can venture into a project, even one that they want to do. If their weeks are packed, saving a half or even full weekend can be helpful. (#1 counts as unstructured time.)

3. ADJUST HOMEWORK

If their homework is repetitive and tedious, and they are able to somehow communicate that they understand the work, ask their teacher if they can have less homework, or show their work in other ways. Remember to make this as easy on the teacher as possible.

They are busy (and underpaid!)

4. WELCOME TECHNOLOGY

This is the way our children learn and play. Their brains are fast. Sometimes learning from YouTube videos or documentaries suits them more than reading a textbook. Especially if there are executive functioning challenges.

Listening to audiobooks might engage them more than reading books, and they may remember stories or information better that way. Welcome their way of learning.

Help them to understand how to fact check and to do things like navigating comments, so they do not become overwhelmed. These are skills they will need in life anyway.

Additionally, video and online gaming can have its value.* We don't know what the jobs of the future will look like, but I'm pretty sure that brain surgeons will be using technology to operate (if they aren't already).

Multiplayer gaming can promote social skills.

5. GET OUTSIDE WITH YOUR VISUAL-SPATIAL LEARNER

Visual-spatial children need to move and be in nature. The truth is that we all need nature, but VS learners who tend to be highly sensitive need nature to soften the harshness of the world so they can unwind, recharge, and reconnect to themselves.

6. BE AWARE OF HOW SCHOOL WORK CAN IMPACT BEHAVIOR AND MENTAL HEALTH

If your child is having behavior issues, or is showing signs of depression, and you suspect that it is due to a mismatched school setting, seek help from professionals who understand this population.

Additionally, if you do nothing else for your VS child, understanding them will go a long way. Your relationship, (and any adult in their life who understands them), is going to be helpful.

If you are able to do one thing on this list, you are helping them.

7. REFRAME THEIR SITUATION AND SIDE COACH

If you are able, understanding your VS child and in turn, helping them to understand themselves in the context of a mostly non-visual spatial world can go a long way.

If this is something you will never in a million years understand, seek outside help from a professional who truly understands this. These kids are often their own worst critics.

Instead of "there's something wrong with me, I don't fit in," you can help them to understand "this isn't the best educational fit for me. They can't teach me in the way I learn."

Find your own words that represent your understanding of this.

Children know the truth when they hear it. Remind them that school doesn't need to be the only place where they learn (and therefore judge their ability to learn.) It may take only a few conversations to internalize this understanding, with the goal being for them to be able to understand themselves, and when age-appropriate, to advocate for themselves.

8. HELP THEM FIND THEIR PEOPLE

Are they crazy about coding, sewing, or even Dungeons and Dragons? Find a group if you can. Or you may need to connect them with one important friend.

Have a quirky, visual-spatial aunt or neighbor down the street? Or a random kid they connected with at their tae kwon do class, but they live an hour away? Welcome these relationships and make the drive if you can.

The world is changing. I believe our visual-spatial learners are wired for the future.

Many of them are concerned with, and ready to solve many of the world's problems that most of us can't even imagine there are solutions to. Meeting them where they are at and helping them navigate their education while holding on to their gifts is key to helping them reach their potential.

These kids are amazing. I think we can all agree that we want them to be happy, to continue to grow, and ultimately to become contributing members of our planet.

*Signs of depression and anxiety, including overuse of video gaming, are important to understand more deeply. Please seek professional help when needed.

Making Sense of Your Gifted Child's Diagnosis: A Review of *Misdiagnosis and Dual Diagnosis of Gifted Children* and Adults

I'm in a therapy session with Peter (not his real name), a high-school-aged boy. His depression is palpable. He's assuring me that he's fine and can work harder to keep up his grades. While his ADHD meds helped him get his homework done for a while - he told me, while on the meds, "I could stay up all night," - they have since stopped working. He tells me that sometimes he "just can't focus," but he's not able to answer when or why that might happen. When I ask Peter about his artwork, he gets excited; the room seems to lighten. With pride, he talks to me a bit about the process he goes through in creating his work; a lot of the planning is in his head. It becomes clear that with his artwork he is able to focus.

When we turn to other topics, the room returns to a feeling of fuzzy depression. He's determined to do his homework and get better grades. But his history shows that no matter how much he promises, and how much effort he puts into it, it's unlikely this will happen. He wants to fit in.

As a second grader, Peter went through a variety of tests. The result was that he tested as gifted. He was also diagnosed with depression and ADHD. The diagnoses of ADHD and depression are what stuck. His giftedness was ignored by professionals, and over time, also by his family and himself.

I witness variations on this story often. It is heartbreaking for all, but particularly so for those of us who have seen the gifted fail. We understand what's going wrong, or at least where to start in helping a child get out of depression, but how much is a real pathology? How much is due to an ill-fitting education? How much is due to misunderstandings? I have sat in a room many times with a gifted individual who suffered from lack of understanding of giftedness rather than any other factor. Those of us who are parents of gifted children or who regularly work with gifted children in these types of situations are grateful for James Webb's work in the field of gifted psychology and education.

In *Misdiagnosis and Dual Diagnosis of Gifted Children and Adults*, Webb et al., (see complete reference at the end of this chapter), reaffirm what many of us have found out anecdotally: changing school fit and understanding the quirks that come along with giftedness can remove many struggles:

...as a group, gifted children and adults appear to be at somewhat lower risk (for any disorder) than the population at large — at least if their intellectual, social, and emotional needs are being met to a reasonable degree ... However, there appears to be a significant likelihood of diagnoses of various disorders — as well as misdiagnoses — if there is educational misplacement or lack of family understanding ... Either factor can result in a lack of fit that can create significant stress for these children, as well as for the adults around them.

I would add that, of all the diagnoses your child receives, giftedness is the most important. Any other diagnoses, should there be any, will be better understood through the gifted lens.

CHAPTERS 2 THROUGH 8: DIAGNOSES EXPLAINED AND DIFFERENTIATED FOR THE GIFTED

As a clinician, curious mother, and human, these are my favorite chapters of Webb's book. Here, in a very structured format, traits of disorders and traits of the gifted are compared and contrasted. The authors further illustrate for us with examples of gifted individuals. Of particular interest is that gifted traits that "look like" these disorders are named, providing insights into why a clinician who doesn't understand giftedness may misdiagnose.

I caution parents not to use this as a rule book, nor to try to diagnose your own child, but these chapters can act as a hefty guideline when talking with your child's practitioner about a diagnosis and provides an understanding of the importance of working with a practitioner who is knowledgeable about giftedness.

ADHD

The best example from the above section is of ADHD, the "diagnosis du jour" as Webb would say when speaking. (During lectures, he would often joke that there are trends in diagnoses. Years ago, the "diagnosis du jour" for children was bipolar disorder.) The authors believe that ADHD is over diagnosed in gifted children about 50% of the time. They do, however, emphasize that ADHD does co-occur with giftedness, and sometimes giftedness can mask ADHD symptoms. The book breaks down the three different scenarios using examples, which many will find helpful.

I recommend reading the book cover to cover, especially if you are a clinician. However, if you are a book skimmer, and tend to return to books over time, as many busy parents do, and/or are new to the gifted label, I recommend reading the following topics:

OVEREXCITABILITIES

Children with overexcitabilities are passionate. "When they discover numbers, they may say things like, 'Oh, wow! Nine! What a gorgeous number. Two is so ordinary, but nine!'" With compassion and understanding, the authors explain that gifted people can be intense and sensitive in specific ways. "Their passion and their intensity lead these brighter individuals to be so reactive that their feelings, experiences, or reactions far exceed what one would typically expect." Webb et al. illustrate well how understanding these traits can greatly impact diagnoses.

SENSORY DISORDERS

The authors write, "Simply put, a sensory integration disorder is present when the sensory organ (eye, ear, etc.) works normally, but the experience or perception of the individual is abnormal."

Since we cannot experience what the child experiences, there are many misunderstandings and misdiagnoses when sensory disorders are present. This book briefly presents and sums up some of the ways to recognize this disorder in order to appropriately address the issues with a professional.

LEARNING STYLES: AUDITORY-SEQUENTIAL VS. VISUAL-SPATIAL

In our schools designed for the linear-sequential learner, understanding your child's learning style is extremely helpful to your child's success. I often see visual-spatially dominant children who try hard to fit into the auditory-sequential school system. Their failure to "fit in" can be a contributing factor to depression and/or acting out.

Webb et al. discuss some typical problems that can arise for the visual-spatial learners and why these types of learners can be misdiagnosed.

A helpful chart compares the two types of learners side by side. The auditory-sequential list has traits like: "prefers solving existing problems," and "prefers concrete tasks that have one correct answer." The visual-spatial list has descriptions such as "prefers solving novel or self-generated problems," and "prefers concepts: better at reasoning than at computation."

DEPRESSION

The diagnosis I see most in working with school-age children is depression. Via references throughout the book and the section on depression, Webb et al. express keen awareness of this.

> *…it is not uncommon for gifted children to experience a mild to severe depression related to their educational situation; in some of these children, the depression is moderate to severe if the child is educationally misplaced and if the school is not being responsive to the child's need.*

LACK OF EMPATHY

Gifted children are often misdiagnosed as lacking empathy. Differentiating the many things that can cause that appearance is helpful. Of particular note is the authors' differentiation between lacking tolerance and lacking empathy – something that all parents, teachers, and practitioners should keep in mind. In my practice I know children who were told that they lack empathy, when what they actually have is an acute ability to sense the emotions of others combined with an intensity that they have not learned how to manage. This incorrect belief can be incredibly difficult to undo in my experience.

It is important to note that human beings, gifted or not, are resilient, and if you are reading this and have misunderstood your child, your student, or yourself, know that it's never too late. Read up on giftedness, connect with other gifted parents, and if needed, seek out a therapist or gifted consultant who you resonate with.

If you have a gifted family or work with the gifted, Webb's book is the book to keep on the shelf to return to again and again.

The School Meeting

At the core of what I offer are ways to allow parents to remember to trust their gut. This sounds very simple, but many of us do not in certain situations, especially when dealing with a teacher, professional, or group whom we trust.

Sometimes a communication such as a judgment or perception of our child, or even a solution, may be different than what feels right to us. When your gut tells you something is "off," in a situation involving your child (a judgment, perception, even a solution), this is important information. Not to dismiss the professional whose intention is to help your child, but pay attention to your own input into the process. Use it to take a break, gather information, stop a process, whatever is needed to get clearer on why you are feeling or thinking something different.

Here is an example: During a meeting at my son's school, involving the school psychologist, the special ed teacher (with whom he had never worked), his teacher, the principal, a special ed support person, and a reading specialist, my husband and I were told that he had some behavior issues. While nobody would say it, I felt that they were hinting that he may have ADHD. That my son might have ADHD is not a problem for me. I believe accurate diagnoses are important and often bring a relief because you know what direction to go in to get your child help. What I wanted was to get to the bottom of what was going on, to find the cause of his behavior. But something was telling me that things weren't adding up. The meeting felt like things were going too fast. (This was the first time I was hearing any feedback of this sort, although I knew something was up and had observed many a day on the school yard to see how things were going, but found nothing wrong.) I also had the strong impression that something had been decided about my son without my input—as though they had agreed on something about him, had put him in some category—but that they didn't know him well enough to do so. At the same time, they had observed him in situations I hadn't, which was information I wanted. To me, this feeling in the room as though something about him was already decided was strong. I was upset and felt like the I was being perceived as the "defensive mom" in the meeting. What I needed, I realized later was to slow things down, gather information, and work as a team. I wanted to know why he hadn't had this problem in previous classrooms. What was different about this year?

After leaving the meeting, giving it some thought, and talking to friends, I felt clearer and somewhat less defensive. At the next meeting, I would ask questions that I hadn't quite had time to formulate to ask in the first meeting. As a psychotherapist, I knew from the *Diagnostic and Statistical Manual of Mental Health Disorders* (DSM) of the time that if you were to diagnose a child with ADHD, the child had to show symptoms in more than one location (for example, at school and at home, or at school and at the babysitters). I think I had said, "but he isn't always like this!" (fulfilling the defensive mom role), during the first meeting, but only received blank stares. I needed some specific examples.

I thought of scenarios to illustrate this by the next meeting. At the time my son was writing his version of the eighth novel in the Harry Potter series. He couldn't write or read fast enough, so he would dictate a few pages while I wrote them down, then draw pictures, then dictate again. One day he did this for five hours straight. I am not exaggerating. My husband left to go to the store twice during that time, and I had to eat at some point, but my son did not want to stop. This didn't seem to fit the description of the unfocused child that the teachers had described to me. He was also in a Harry Potter after school class (seeing a theme here?) at the time. This was a small class of five students where they enacted scenes from the books. He had no behavior problems in this class. I brought both of these examples up at the next meeting. They seemed very interested in this, and one day I saw the special ed person visiting the Harry Potter class. What I brought to the table was a very different view of how they were beginning to see my child.

Needless to say, it didn't work out at this school for different reasons, but my point is that in our work as parents in supporting our children, trusting our own instincts about them, and figuring out how to bring this to the table is just as important as the professionals we put our trust in, if not more.

Developmental Milestones of Executive Functioning in Differently Tuned-In Kids

Executive functioning is the ability to organize, plan, understand time, and basically fit one's inner world into the linear sequence of the outer world. Of all the quirky behaviors that our children can have, the most exasperating for parents and teachers to deal with relate to executive functioning. It's hard to not feel judgmental when your child has lost his jacket for the 4th time, and it's still the beginning of winter! Additionally, most of us were reprimanded for such behavior when we were young. We all know that our anger only shames a child who simply cannot remember his jacket, even if he tries, and cares very deeply about how his behavior is perceived.

So often the differently tune-in brain, which is not wired like the neurotypical brain, does not have the ability to perform many executive functioning tasks until around age 12. There are some who say the brain takes another leap in executive functioning ability around age 20, and most people agree that for everyone, the prefrontal cortex is fully developed by age 25 to 30. These ages are important in helping differently tuned-in children because it allows us to manage our expectations in a way that gives children the space and guidance they need to experiment with their executive functioning skills in a healthy way.

Often, it seems that once we come up with a label, any label, it seems to define a child. Just by using a word, it is hard to move away from it. The child's abilities as perceived by adults and then the child, can become stagnant and attached to the word, when in reality, our abilities and disabilities, perhaps especially in differently wired children, are quite fluid.

Many differently wired young children cannot memorize the order of the alphabet, know the days of the week, or the order of months, but by the teen years have more command over these abilities.

Knowing when they may have additional abilities in this area can allow a parent/teacher to be more patient in the earlier years, and kindly challenge the child's executive functioning skills at these crucial stages. It will take some trial and error to discover if the skills are beginning to show themselves, but the expectation that they may have them can open doors.

Of course, nothing happens overnight. If you lose your patience when it comes to your child's inability to brush his teeth in less than an hour, most of us can relate (we are only human!). Take a breath and try to be kinder next time. Being honestly interested in a child's inner process in terms of executive functioning can be enlightening for an adult who had previously given up all hope. A child can become very proud of their new skills, especially when there isn't too much shame attached to them to begin with. Good luck!

SPECIFIC CHALLENGES OF UNDERSTANDING GIFTED BOYS

In my world working with gifted homeschoolers, 2e children in gifted schools, and being a mother to one, I am seeing a pattern with some of the boys. It's a feedback loop that seems to start in a typical school, but when strengthened, can seep into the relationships with parents and even educators. Here's how it works:

The boy has a behavior that is understandably misunderstood. It is a behavior that scares us. It can look like bullying or something violent, biting sarcasm or even just a little meanness. The adults react (or overreact) and the child, in turn, reacts to the adults, and these behaviors grow stronger and can manifest in more and more extreme ways. As can be expected, the adult's reactions then become stronger as well. Because the boy feels that no one has faith in his goodness anymore, eventually he begins to internalize the adults' perceptions of him and sees himself as a "bad kid." Even when the adults are not saying, "you're a bad kid," or even when they are saying the opposite, the child knows by their reactions how he's being perceived. He feels that he is essentially bad. If the feedback loop continues, he may fall into a self-fulfilling prophecy and by high school perceives himself as a hopeless case. He throws in the towel and begins not to care.

But, let's rewind and take a look at a first-grade boy who is just beginning this pattern.

Mathew, (name has been changed), a first grader in a typical school, scored extremely high on the emotional overexcitabilities (OEs) as well as physical and intellectual. His behaviors related to this OE were beginning to show up in more obvious ways.

Mathew's high sensitivity shows up in ways that are interpreted in reverse – as being low-sensitive and uncaring. In fact, he cares very much how he is perceived, and especially how his parents see him, as well as his peers and adults whom he admires. But he hides this through silly behavior and sometimes anger when his parents become upset at him. In addition, he has a certain rigidity over how people should behave. He has a strong sense of social justice, and when he sees anyone treated unfairly, especially by adults, his feelings of anger are quite big. When combined with his yet-to-be developed ability to see a problem from another's perspective, it can lead to huge misunderstandings about his intentions.

In one incident, when a boy in Mathew's class was in trouble for hitting another child and faced with expulsion, Mathew became very upset. According to Mathew, the child who was hit had said something extremely hurtful to the boy who hit him. In Mathew's eyes, the teachers overreacted to the incident, shaming the child who did the hitting. Parents were involved, and boys were asked not to interact with the boy who did the hitting. Mathew felt both boys were in the wrong. In fact, he later interviewed the boys, and both admitted to being in the wrong.

Mathew's mother tried to explain that physically hurting someone at a school has to be taken seriously by the school – it's "just the way it is, especially in the public school system." This made Mathew madder. That an arbitrary rule would overrule a social justice issue was his hot button. He didn't have the emotional space to step back and see the problem as a larger issue, as most adults reading this probably can.

His reaction was strong, and mostly in his body, as though he needed to fight someone. He said he wanted to fight the school. His mother tried to explain how things are done, and that he wouldn't be solving anything were he to take action in an angry way. To this, he cited various tyrannical governments and asked what the difference was between them and his school. (Yes, this is first grade, but maybe you know the type?)

At one point, one of his friends reported that Mathew had talked of blowing up the school. When his mother asked Mathew about the people who would be hurt, he replied that he would make sure no one was hurt. Mathew has never carried out a plan such as this, and his mother was certain that his words were from his realm of imaginary. It was his way of expressing frustration. In our current atmosphere of fear of security in our schools, Mathew's words understandably trigger alarm from adults — which tends to make him respond even more strongly. From the outside, Mathew's behavior might be labeled as sociopathic by some, but in this case, it is his OE that needs to be understood and tempered by the adults. This type of behavior could turn into defiance after some time. Some of this depends on how the adults treat the behavior, and of course, some depends on the boy.

After speaking with me and understanding how Mathew's OEs are impacting his ability to respond to situations like this, Mathew's mother wasn't sure she could help the school understand where Mathew's rebelliousness was coming from. This was a busy public school, with bigger problems to deal with.

Knowing that Mathew's mother and teacher had a good relationship and that Mathew had found this teacher's daily mindfulness exercises relaxing, I suggested they have a meeting. There, Mathew's mother explained her son's motivation behind the threat and succeeded in getting his teacher to understand the depth of Mathew's feelings around the perceived injustice to his classmate.

The teacher was able to have a heart-to-heart discussion with Mathew from which things shifted for Mathew. While he continues to be an advocate for social justice, he has dropped his fantasy of blowing up the school. Mathew's mother told me that his teacher had a lesson plan on Martin Luther King, Jr, and explained how he had been a fierce advocate for social justice, "like Mathew is."

While this is likely to be an ongoing theme in Mathew's life, I truly believe that his teacher, in her mindful and non-reactive way, was instrumental in helping him through one major level of understanding, not only by what she said but by how she handled and responded to him. It took great skill for her to accept some responsibility in understanding the cause of Mathew's stress and to change *her* reactivity. My hope is that Mathew can internalize his teacher's ability to react thoughtfully when under stress.

In this way, a mindful adult can help interrupt this feedback loop that many of our boys get into. The emphasis is on the feedback loop – the reactivity becomes stronger and more defensive as the child feels the authority figure's negative reaction to him. This is a common conundrum for a child with this type of intensity.

6 Signs Your Preschooler May Be Gifted and Why It's Important to Know

I had no idea what giftedness meant when I had my son. So, when he spoke his first word at 4 months, I thought I was hearing things. One day, when he was two years old, I was nervous about something. He said, "Mommy, just breathe." I had no context. I knew he was special, but I didn't connect it to the word "gifted."

What most people don't know about giftedness is that it comes with different wiring and different psychological and medical needs. Gifted individuals can have one or all of the following: extreme sensitivities, intensities, creative and intellectual drives, and perfectionism. The more highly gifted, the more extreme these traits can be, paradoxically, making it more difficult to identify giftedness. (Most standard testing does not test into the higher level of testing.) The child's struggles usually become noticeable once they are in the school setting. Boys often act out (getting the most attention), while girls tend to use their gifts to fit in. The inner world of the gifted child can be much larger than he knows how to express, and sometimes learning how to be in the world can be difficult. While many people associate the term "special needs" with children who have developmental or learning challenges, it means only that a child has "special needs" and gifted children are a special needs population.

As a result, we as parents, need to know what to watch for, when, and have some tools to identify and address what may be going on with your children. The most important thing is that you understand your child.

Today I coach and consult parents of exceptional children and give talks at schools, but when my own child was going through some difficult school years, I had already completed what I thought was a well-rounded training in the field of psychology. I had a master's degree in Counseling Psychology, with two years of post-graduate training (because I wanted to make sure I wasn't missing anything,) and was a licensed Marriage and Family Therapist. In all that time, in school or in the field, the term "gifted" never entered into my training, even though special needs can come along with giftedness. Most professionals working with children have not had training in exceptional children.

It's not their fault. It's just often not part of the curriculum.

One of my major goals in my work is to help parents identify their gifted children early enough to get them headed in the right direction (keeping in mind that it's never too late!)

With the understanding that nothing is written in stone as relates to the gifted, here are 6 signs to watch for that may indicate that your preschooler is gifted:

1. READS OR IS INTERESTED IN BOOKS EARLY

Gifted children, even those who cannot read, often show interest in books very early. Before my son could walk, he would take a book off the shelf and try to open it and turn the pages. Most gifted children are voracious readers.

There is one caveat to be aware of: in my world, there are many highly to profoundly gifted people with unusual vision issues. I'm not sure how this is related, but I'm hopeful there will be studies. Though we had my son's vision tested three times throughout his childhood, he wasn't correctly diagnosed until second grade when we took him to a developmental optometrist. After vision therapy, he began to read. Key point: interest in books.

2. EARLY LANGUAGE

These kids are able to articulate things that many adults cannot. When my son was 14 months old, I was considering putting him in preschool and going back to work. I remember a day where I was particularly torn and distraught. He looked at me and said, "I just want my mommy to be happy." That was a big wow moment.

Another caveat: A child may have apraxia (a speech sound disorder) or dysarthria (a difficulty with strength or coordination of the speech muscles), which prevents him from articulating, but this does not necessarily mean there isn't understanding. A four-year-old couldn't speak (and was in speech therapy), but I could see his eyes moving across the page of a book, as though reading. You may be able to see signs that the child is understanding complex language and ideas, even though they can't speak.

3. HAS A CONSTANT DRIVE TO UNDERSTAND, EXPLORE, CREATE, AND REMEMBER ODD FACTS IN THEIR AREAS OF INTEREST

Gifted children are always doing something, talking about something, or learning something. Hello, exhausted parent. They can have very specific interests that last a lifetime, or they may go deeply into a topic for months. My son, like many children, had his dinosaur phase, his deep-sea-creature phase, his machines phase, his I'm-a-scientist-and-I'm-going-to-experiment-all-day phase (that was so fun to clean up after), the phase where our house felt like a rain forest because there were toy animals and bugs on the floors, countertops, and walls. It's like each mess had a theme.

During his deep-sea-creature phase, at age three, he had been attending a Spanish-speaking preschool. While he wouldn't speak Spanish at home, we were told that he spoke it at school. One day, while looking at a book about sea creatures at a friend's house, I overheard him correct the Spanish of a Spanish-speaking family friend. The adult told me later that what my son had used was actually a more precise Spanish word for a species than he, as a native-Spanish-speaking person was using. (As a side note, many gifted people are interested in what is hidden from plain sight. Things like what goes on under the surface of the ocean, the architecture of burrowing animals' homes, fossils, or even the elephant in the room.)

These moments when we notice brilliance can be fun and should be cherished. But as parents of a highly to profoundly gifted child know, these children also have their challenges. If you see these signs in your child at such a young age, take notice. It may not be so cute in a few years if they get bored and become a bad fit for their education. Early intervention is important.

4. RELATES TO ADULTS EASILY

Often, gifted children exhibit an ability to interact well with adults. They can use language more akin to that of adults and talk about things at a deeper level. This is somewhat logical if their cognitive and interest skills are advanced for their age group. Does your child have long conversations with, and seek out that scientist-neighbor, more than kids his own age? Encourage the friendship. Who says we have to hang out with people our own age all the time.

The other side to this is that a gifted child may be socially out of sync with her peers. While much of the emphasis for these children, starting from preschool is to help them "get along" better with their same-age peers, finding peers who are wired like them is going to be more helpful initially. As they grow into an understanding of themselves and why they are different, they will be better equipped to socially interact with same-age peers.

5. CAN HOLD ATTENTION TO A TASK LONGER THAN NORMAL WHEN ENGAGED

Gifted kids can get into a book or video, create a project such as writing a story or drawing artwork for hours with a sense of deep concentration. At the same time, giftedness can also bring intense perfectionism and frustration at not being able to master a task that they can so easily envision. Once older, most gifted children prefer to go deeply into a topic that they enjoy. These same children may appear inattentive in a typical school setting, and sometimes even as early as preschool.

One baby I observed could turn over onto his back, but not the other way around. As he tried to turn back the other way, he would get extremely frustrated. So much so that his usually patient mom had to control herself not to help him flip the other way. His frustration felt bigger than most babies'.

Once he was on his belly, he arched his back so that he could see in front of himself. Positioned halfway between a rug and a hardwood floor, he looked at the floor and back to the rug. With deep concentration, his body struggling to keep his head up, he patted the hardwood floor and then the rug, then watched and appeared to be listening to the sound intently. His eyes were very intent and focused. It was as though he was conducting a scientific experiment on the difference in texture and volume, using sound, and sight between the two.

The person assessing your child will need to know that they have this ability. Often, children who are in settings that cause different behavior, or are being asked to do tasks not in line with their ability, (above or below, when other children do them easily), will cause behavior that looks like an inability to focus.

6. SEEMS MORE SENSITIVE THAN OTHERS, SHOWING EMPATHY IN NOTEWORTHY WAYS

I'll touch on this complex issue in later articles, but I find that some highly to profoundly gifted children are not only highly sensitive people but are *empaths*. This means that they are having a *felt sense* of what others are going through. (For example, the baby in a room full of babies, who begins crying when he hears another baby crying.) They become *empathic* when they can understand this felt sense and help the other.

I don't really know why I made this poor decision, but one Saturday I took my two-year-old son to IKEA. It was Saturday, so of course, it was crowded and loud.

My son had a meltdown. He was inside the large part of the cart and insisted on standing up as I was trying to whisk us out of the store. Needless to say, I wasn't at my best at this point. Loud places are too much for both of us. When we got outside, heading toward the parking garage, I saw a little girl, about four years old, running behind us. My son was still standing in the cart, crying and red-faced. This girl ran up beside our cart, reached up over the bars and held out her hand to him. He slowed his crying, looked at her, held her hand, and sat down. Their fingers met through the bars. Little by little, his sobs subsided. He looked intently at her and listened to what she was whispering to him. Afterward, he fell asleep in the car on the drive home. Peace.

If you haven't noticed already, these kids are a bunch of paradoxes. While they can often stay focused on a task or interest for long periods of time, many can take longer to learn tasks like cleaning up (boring!) or brushing teeth. Additionally, the sensitivities can cause them to shut down in the areas they are sensitive. While my son can tell me how the birds sound differently from one place to another, he can sometimes lose it in a loud, crowded place (like IKEA on a Saturday), because he is taking in the noise more intensely.

These sensitivities can sometimes make a gifted individual appear *insensitive*, such as the child who doesn't easily make eye contact. For some, making eye contact is a very intense, even private act.

Once you've noticed signs of giftedness, make sure to seek help from professionals who know the difference between the gifted ranges and how this impacts all areas, not just education. It's not unusual for me to get calls from parents of high-school-age children who have had a trail of different diagnoses for their child. Understanding how your child learns and engages with the world as early as possible is the best gift you can give them.

How to Obtain Proper Testing for the Exceptional Learner

Alex's mother called me because she was confused about what her second-grader was going through. She had pulled him out of school because his behavior and emotional health seemed to be getting worse, and she was beginning to suspect that he was "just different" than other learners, but couldn't quite put her finger on what was going on. She was also concerned that he might have some social and learning challenges. While she saw improvements in her son emotionally, now that he was home, she was exhausted. She informed me that she had Alex take a neuropsychological evaluation, but that they were not able to test further because he was refusing whenever he was required to look at paper. She said that he was jumpy during the test, and wouldn't let her leave his side. She was perplexed that he was given a score, as she didn't see that Alex was able to complete the testing.

To make matters more confusing, Alex's mom had taken him to an occupational therapist who said that Alex had weakened hand muscles and dysgraphia (inability to write). When Alex asked his mom what that meant, he told her he would no longer write, since it "wasn't (his) skillset". His mother told me that there had been times when he could write almost perfect letters, but not usually. Also, when he drew animals, something her son loved, he could draw very detailed and accurate lines on the page, using cross-hatching at times. This didn't seem to fit with the diagnosis of weakened muscles in his hands.

When parents get the sense that their differently tuned-in children's abilities go far beyond what they demonstrate in school, or when the child is showing increasing frustration and low self-esteem, this is when most parents start to wonder what is going on. Parents need answers, and often turn to multiple specialists as Alex's mother did. To say that Alex's mom and Alex were in a high state of stress at this time is an understatement. This stress can impact testing outcomes, and the testing can add to the stress and sense of urgency.

Alex's story is a pretty typical one, with several seemingly unconnected moving parts. What they needed was a compassionate person who could truly see Alex and assess him in a clear, holistic way, even though neither mother nor son was at their best at this time.

I used my 3-phase protocol to assess and treat Alex. The first phase was the initial assessment, the second involved some treatments and, in Alex's case, educational fit, and the third was a follow-up and reassessment. Significant improvements were seen by 6 months, and Alex had more fine-tuned, continued improvements socially and academically over the years. Today, Alex is in high school and thriving. His parents contact me from time to time for help-- for their son and their family.

The seemingly unrelated symptoms in differently wired children are better assessed and treated holistically, as they all impact each other.

For the differently wired child, you will want to find a professional who understands the following aspects and how each one can impact the others: sensory issues, sensitivities, intensities, strong will, executive functioning/ADHD, giftedness and twice-exceptionality, visual-spatial learning styles, anxiety, depression, and perfectionism. Finding the right person--quickly-- is important. If you feel comfortable, then so will your child, and with comfort and ease comes a more accurate assessment and outcome. Good luck!

.

How Can I Tell Sensory Issues From Other Issues?

Sensory processing issues can be misunderstood and misdiagnosed as a number of things, most commonly ADHD, and anxiety disorders. In my opinion, it is necessary to rule out any sensory issues or address them as thoroughly as possible before considering other diagnoses.

Does your child seem agitated and is he agitating to be around? Or conversely, does she avoid being with others, and seems to shut down when she would really like to connect? Usually our kids want to do things right — to listen, sit still, control their impulses, be a member of the group — but sometimes they're unable to. This can be frustrating for children, especially when they are blamed for such behavior.

In my practice, I see many kids like this. They appear to have signs of ADHD, but it could be something entirely different. Some of the behaviors may be part of these children's hardwiring that comes with exceptionalities, but the sudden outbursts, the inability to control impulses, or the intolerance of any noise in the room could indicate sensory processing issues. Exceptional children may be more likely to have Sensory Processing Disorders (SPDs) simply because they are more sensitively wired. I highly recommend getting children checked for sensory issues before, or in conjunction with gifted testing, or any other testing. (If they do have ADHD, for example, it's best to clear out sensory issues to accurately get help for the ADHD. If they have anxiety, you may see that cut down by thoroughly addressing the sensory issues.)

Sensory processing issues are often misunderstood. They have more to do with how the brain processes the senses rather than the senses themselves. Children with sensory processing issues can be either sensory seekers or sensory avoiders. For example, a child may make loud sounds in order to hear the reverberation in her head that she is craving because her brain has not registered certain pitches of sound. Alternatively, a child might find the seams in her socks are intolerable because her brain is receiving too much stimulation. Both of these could be going on within the same child.

To further complicate things, standard testing of visual and hearing exams won't necessarily indicate problems. In fact, visual and auditory issues are often missed. Most exams for vision and hearing at schools and in the doctor's office do not test for deeper visual and auditory issues.

If sensory issues are found, addressing these issues with appropriate therapies as thoroughly as possible is important. I find integrative therapies to be quicker and more effective than occupational therapy. Vision therapy is quite effective when followed through and done regularly. I have seen a child who was very resistant to vision therapy, (because it made him nauseous), suddenly become more open to it and advance significantly after addressing his vestibular issues first. The correct sensory therapies will reconnect wiring in the brain that is out of balance, solving the problem at its core. Only once that's done can you or a professional see more clearly if there are other issues. (A child cannot receive tutoring for dyslexia while there are unresolved vision issues – that is like teaching a child to run without first mending their broken leg.)

An example is Jane (name has been changed). She seems jumpy, has difficulty reading, and tends to lack an appropriate "space bubble" around her, (she gets a little too close to friends and knocks things over accidentally.) She consistently tested as having 20/20 vision, but through testing with a certified developmental optometrist, it was discovered that she has esotropia (one eye turned in at times), and tracking issues (had a difficult time finding words on a page when looking from left to right). Once her issues were identified and she received vision therapy, she was able to control herself. Her mother reported that she was "so much more grounded." While she may still have ADHD, she appears much less agitated and has her self-esteem back because she's no longer agitating to others!

Another child, Dennis, was very loud at inappropriate times, seemed agitated internally, especially in noisy environments, and was annoying to others around him. At times he requested to be in a room by himself; at others, he joined the group but became loud and aggressive. Similarly, his mom reported that he would begin yelling when a blender or vacuum was turned on. The paradox is that he may have been yelling to match the noise he perceived in order to tolerate it: he yelled as a coping mechanism because the loud noise made him feel overwhelmed. While he was thought to have a problem with his ears, he tested as having good hearing. After proper testing, it turned out Dennis had Central Auditory Processing Disorder (CAPD), which made him unable to filter noises properly. He heard noises from far away as if they were close up, and unless he was looking at his mother's lips, he didn't hear her when she was standing directly in front of him. His brain needed to be retrained to hear appropriately. After completing auditory therapy, he became more grounded, no longer shouting at odd times. Now, when his mother talks to him and he "doesn't hear," he jokes, "oh, now I hear you, I was just ignoring you." At least now it is his choice and he's kept his sense of humor.

An important point to make here is that these therapies can be intense for some kids and can temporarily exacerbate behaviors. At one point, Dennis stopped auditory therapy because he was very resistant to it. At about the same time his challenging behavior escalated. I urged the parent to continue the therapy, but with someone who knew how to regulate it according to what he could tolerate, and who could help balance his system while he was going through it.

As a parent of a 2e child, I know that all of the therapies and diagnoses can be overwhelming. While we want the best for our children, many of our brains and budgets are overstretched.

> *As someone who has been trained to diagnose children in the mental health setting, I know that sensory issues can look like any number of pathologies to professionals. I urge parents to consider sensory issues while looking into other diagnoses such as ADHD and anxiety.*

Considering and addressing sensory issues, rather than being an additional step, can actually solve many behavioral issues more efficiently and properly than more common treatments. It may lead to a more grounded, peaceful child who can manage his world. It may even make your world more manageable.

Why is High-Achieving Synonymous with Being Gifted? Because We Didn't Listen to This Woman

It was 100 years ago that Leta Hollingworth, a female psychologist, coined the term "gifted." In her research of, and work with children who were assessed using the Stanford-Binet tests, she realized that the highly and profoundly gifted had certain vulnerabilities. She wrote about it; she studied it. Her objective was to look not only at academic achievement but at the whole child: their emotional, aesthetic, cognitive, and affective development. In her book, *Gifted Children: Their Nature and Nurture*, written in 1926, she pointed out issues that some gifted children face such as, but not limited to, problems with school work (it's boring and doesn't match their needs), adjustment to classmates, difficulties at play and conformity, and the special problems of the gifted girl (she has "strong preferences for activities that are hard to follow on account of [her] sex, which is inescapable.")

As most of us parents do, Hollingworth looked at the heart, mind, body, and spirit to assess what gifted children needed. She observed that highly to profoundly gifted children learned and developed asynchronously, and emphasized the need for flexibility in their instruction. She clearly understood that not giving these children what they needed in an education, including the proper emotional support, would limit their abilities to achieve. She stated that the purpose of the teacher was to "act as a facilitator of learning and of emotional growth, to assist with the problems arising out of the disparities between mental and chronological age."

For most of us in the gifted field, or who are homeschooling, or who are trying to find the most suitable path for our gifted children, we have observed many of the things Hollingworth did. Yet, despite Hollingworth identifying these issues a century ago, we've had to figure these out on our own, sometimes after many years of confusion and suffering within the current paradigm of our psychology and education systems. We think our discoveries must be new because they haven't reached most professionals in mental health and education: those we look to in order to educate, diagnose, and guide us with our children.

So, how is it that it feels like we're just discovering the real needs of the gifted, given that this was 100 years ago?

In the 1800s, the era before Hollingworth, the view on high intelligence was that it "… can only be proven once a man is dead, in looking at his awards and accomplishments." As Linda Silverman has said, "It's kind of hard to give a dead man a good gifted education."

In the few years following Hollingworth's death, some of her research students followed through on her work. However, the patriarchal system of the time valued what we can see, measure, prove, and achieve—typically masculine values—over understanding processes, motivation, and what is underneath — feminine values. Achievement remained the only yardstick to measure intellect and giftedness. Even the "Stanford" of the Stanford-Binet test that was developed by one of her contemporaries and is used frequently now for testing was at one point called "The Stanford *Achievement* Test." The term "gifted," coined by Hollingworth to encompass developmental needs and potential, became synonymous with achievement. (One biography of Hollingworth is aptly named *A Forgotten Voice*.)

I assume that most of you reading this are parents who are homeschooling or are otherwise sacrificing in some way to provide a proper education for your gifted child. Maybe you even went through a period (or still are) of sitting in school meetings where your own judgment about your child was highly questioned because they were not high achievers, at least not in all areas. I'm guessing that most of you are mothers who see the same things in your child that Hollingworth saw in the gifted children she helped and observed many years ago. Patriarchy is very much impacting giftedness today in that mothers bear the primary responsibility of identifying and finding solutions for their gifted children. Whether we are homeschooling or having to stop in at school on a weekly basis, we face limited career choices (and sometimes limited sanity). Our education systems' failure to identify and educate our gifted children is further perpetuating the patriarchy.

In a recent conversation with my husband around women's roles in our culture and in our own household, he said that, had I been the higher salary earner, he would have been the one to quit his job to help our son through the difficult years during which we ultimately discovered our son was exceptionally gifted. But, I reminded him, he didn't see that there were deep and complex problems with our son's fit with the school. He preferred to work through more traditional avenues within the school. And he wasn't sure if our son needed to try harder. How could he solve a problem that he couldn't see? He agreed. So just by virtue of the feminine way of thinking, women are often the ones left to struggle with helping their gifted kids. We are also then, the most qualified to know what's best for them. (While I still see mothers bearing the biggest burden in advocating for their children, more and more, I am meeting fathers who are willing and able to see their child's needs on this deeper level.)

What is striking to me is the amount of talent the world is losing due to the gifted mothers who sacrifice their careers to homeschool or otherwise supervise their child's education when this would not be their choice if there were appropriate educational options.

I know of an epidemiologist, an architect, a lawyer, and many who aren't able to develop their careers. We are missing the heart-centered approaches that women tend to bring to their fields that is so needed in our current climate.

When I watched Oprah's Golden Globe speech of 2018, where she said:

...As we try to navigate these complicated times, ...What I know for sure is this: that speaking your truth is the most powerful tool we all have. And I am especially proud and inspired by all of the women who have felt strong enough and empowered enough to speak up and share their personal stories.

I couldn't help but think of Leta Hollingworth and say that, yes, it's time to listen to women, in all contexts. We're entering a new era. The tides are turning and as we women hear our own voices, we are better able to listen to voices like Hollingworth's from 100 years ago. I am grateful to women in the gifted world who have dared to look beyond achievement and champion a deeper way to assess and support the gifted. Women like Anne Marie Roeper and many others like you and I whose challenge is in stepping outside our current educational and psychological paradigm in order to help our gifted children thrive. I have hope that as we listen to more unheard voices, we are moving toward a better world, not just for the gifted, but for everyone.

Unschooling the Differently Wired

For some of us, when we finally realize our children are somewhere in the highly to profoundly gifted range, and that they need a different education, we cross a line. We must let go of what used to be. We must let go of our own expectations of what our kids' lives would or should be. We may need to let go of certain hopes and dreams we had for them, like sports or whatever we *as* parents thought was important. Most of us have to let go of the idea that our school system will support them (and in turn, us). More importantly, I think, when we let go of the school system, and in the words of my son, "the Prussian military education," we are grieving an old way. We are agreeing to trust our children's innate drive to learn, trusting experts on the highly to profoundly gifted, and the experiences of others – adults who have been through it, the parents working their way through, and especially the voices of our own children.

For most of us, going off the beaten path toward finding an education involves embracing some form of unschooling that suits our child. Unschooling is another term, like "gifted," that can easily be misunderstood. I like *Wikipedia's* description:

"Unschooling students learn through their natural life experiences including play, household responsibilities, personal interests and curiosity, internships and work experience, travel, books, elective classes, family, mentors, and social interaction."

Learning and trusting this path is a process, especially when our culture-at-large, often including extended family and close friends, does not support that. We hear about what is working "over there," our neighbor's kid, or read an article from an expert on how to discipline and hold boundaries, or where our child should be in math at a certain age, and we start doubting our choices again.

This is where things can go wrong. Some parents start and stop the process. Some hold so much doubt that it can sabotage learning, especially from our sensitive kids who sometimes know how we, their parents, feel before we do. In agreeing to unschool, we are agreeing that there is an organic drive to learn, grow, explore; we're trusting in our children. Since most of us didn't have that trust extended to ourselves when we were learning, this can be a hard one. Part of our challenge is in making the space, while also providing what is needed for them to keep growing and learning. This is an art and a science. The relationship with the child and understanding them is the most important thing here. You are providing space: the room for them to figure things out and learn as they want, maybe on their own some of the time, depending on the child. And in addition to providing exposure, you're providing scaffolding, so they can have what they need to grow, much like a plant on a vine needs. Scaffolding is the support for areas where the student is weak, so that they can continue to learn and create at the level they are at. Without this support in a traditional school, they would need to wait, which would stifle many of them.

An example of scaffolding is the child who has difficulty writing, but who has a large capacity for storytelling or journalism. Allowing this child to dictate is a form of giving them space to explore their talent as a "writer" while supporting their challenge of not being able to write with pen and paper. (This can also happen to the engineer or musician, where finding ways to keep going without writing or learning to read music may need to be an option, at least for a while and for some, always.) Translating the creative (science or art) to the linear (writing or even verbal), or vice versa, for some can be debilitating.

My husband is a typical linear learner. He excelled in typical school because his linear way of learning fit the mold. He's also smart and a hard worker. So, in our home, when I had to shift away from traditional education for our son because he was struggling, my husband, a Yale-educated, Ph.D. economist, had a really hard time. For years. This was painful. He had to trust me as I trusted the process.

When I homeschooled my son, I came to learn through trial and (lots of) error and through hearing stories from other gifted homeschoolers that unschooling is all that will work for him. It helped to have him assessed and for me to be validated in what I found organically to be true: a typical education will not work for him.

We eventually found a school for highly to profoundly gifted twice exceptional learners. I could tell it was going to work when my son didn't want to leave after our first visit. And because I knew from experience that unschooling from someone who deeply understood him was the only thing that would work. Notice the "Unschool" in the title. My husband still cringes at the word. He associates school with learning, and therefore hears "not learning" in "unschooling." (Whereas I associate unschooling with allowing learning to happen.) Basically, we were going to have someone else unschool our son. The money struggles aside, this was so helpful in building the trust my husband needed.

In the example I gave above of scaffolding, that is my son. To an outside observer (and still, often to me), he can look as though he is doing nothing for months at a time. It can be difficult to watch. There just isn't any tangible product coming home. Nada. I like to compare it to a plant taking root in the earth. We can't see it, but we learn to trust over time that it is happening.

Recently my son started writing a novel (by dictation, but he rereads it in bits to edit) about pirates. The wording exceeds grade level, (he is 11), the relationships are interesting, he uses humor, and you are compelled to continue to read. I am not surprised. I've heard him tell me stories; I hear his humor. While I'm glad he got his story on paper; it feels natural. For my husband, it's as though this novel came out of the blue. I can tell he is surprised and a little verklempt. Suddenly in this product, he can see his son's talent, hard work, and even trusts this crazy unschooling process a bit more.

Trusting the unschooling/scaffolding approach can be especially challenging because there isn't much validation from the world at large, especially when you hit a rough patch. For many of these kids, going for months without seeming to want a new challenge can be hard to watch. The urge to "make" them learn can be strong. Watching their process non-judgmentally, while perceiving what is really going on can be helpful.

Just remember, these kids keep learning on the weekends, evenings, and during the summer. Once hooked on an interest, they sometimes learn a curriculum in a few days that is planned for a year or more.

Trusting the larger picture process is what will be helpful, as well as trusting other parents who have seen the light at the end of the tunnel, their stories, what worked and didn't work, as well as administration and experts who DO get it.

Lately, I've been comparing the process of grieving to the process of learning. In my own process of writing this article, I have found myself returning to deep feelings of grief. You see, my sister died six weeks ago. She had been fighting cancer for a few years, and as valiantly as she struggled, this was a battle she wasn't able to win. For some reason, I feel deeper in my grief now than in the days after she died. I don't understand why. I feel there are ways our culture expects us to grieve, and I try to check myself against that expectation, trying to live up to some idea of "normal" grieving. My mind wants to understand it all, but mostly my heart asks for less judgment. It doesn't matter. All that matters is that I allow myself to grieve. There is nothing wrong with me. There is some voice inside that wants me to trust the process, as painful and as confusing as it is, to give it space, to nurture and love it as it comes out, and let it go. I can't help but make the connection to the trust our children need from us in their innate desire to learn.

Allowing our children to have their space, where we parents step back and get out of the way, is hard. We mourn, and grieve the old, traditional ways; we periodically question ourselves. But if we trust that our children have an intrinsic desire to learn and create, as well as the process they need in order to do this, and keep a watchful eye with love, and allow the natural process to happen, the light at the end of the tunnel will come.

How to Deschool an Exceptional Learner

WHAT IS DESCHOOLING?

Deschooling is the process of allowing a student to abstain from any school or learning-related activities. The objective is to allow the child's intrinsic motivation to learn to return.

While it is easy to understand deschooling in terms of "no school" for a length of time, (and sometimes this is all that is needed,) what is more difficult to understand (and to do!) is the nuance of integrating the twice-exceptional student back into learning. I find that most children will naturally do *some* learning while being deschooled. This integration is crucial to the student's success and is best done using a combination of deschooling and unschooling.

WHY WOULD I NEED TO DESCHOOL MY CHILD?

Deschooling is necessary when a child has experienced school trauma — any intellectual, social, mental, or physical harm within the school setting. The nature and length of the trauma the child has endured impacts the amount of time he needs to deschool, from a few months to a few years.

WHAT IS THE DIFFERENCE BETWEEN UNSCHOOLING AND DESCHOOLING?

Deschooling differs from unschooling but works nicely with it. Unschooling is a method of schooling that follows the child's interest in connection with real life and the real world around them. It can include travel, cooking, watching documentaries, having a mentor, and even traditional instruction and classes.

Both unschooling and deschooling involve a break from the traditional school setting and assume that the child has an intrinsic desire to learn. There usually isn't one magical day when deschooling ends; there is an art and science to knowing when and how to introduce education again. Unschooling works well with deschooling because there is room to understand when to back off, when to drop seeds of thought, and when to allow the child to rise to a challenge, but it can be accomplished in any educational setting with willing adults.

WHAT DO I NEED TO KNOW ABOUT DESCHOOLING?

Not feeling like you belong to a group, not feeling capable, feeling bored (and confused about that boredom), in addition to related issues such as sensory issues, can cause a child to act out in rage or feel deep depression. So many of the parents who I help are in the midst of helping their child out of this. It takes parents and teachers to believe in them in order for them to believe in themselves again. Deschooling *with trust in the process* is a large piece of this puzzle. The paradox here is that deschooling can cause more anxiety for parents who are new to homeschooling or alternative schooling than any other factor.

Because twice-exceptional students are often misidentified as being "behind" the performance level in some or all areas that a traditional school expects, the prospect of deschooling seems to the parents be going in the wrong direction. Additionally, these students can have challenges such as autism, ADHD, or sensory issues. And the tip of the iceberg is that these very same students are often bored to tears because the subject areas that they are very interested in are not being explored in the capacity they crave (if at all). This seemingly paradoxical mix is why traditional school doesn't work and is why a new direction is needed.

Deschooling is the transition to this new way of learning, and inherently involves a big leap of faith. It requires that the adults let go of any outcome in one or all subject areas and invest in discovering how the child learns. The paradox (so many paradoxes!) is that, in letting go of an outcome, the adult is making space for the child to return to the subject on their own terms. Easy to understand, hard to do!

The most important element in allowing the child to heal and to come to learn on their own is the adult's trust in the process and in the fact that the child has an intrinsic desire to learn.

Sometimes the stress or doubts the adult has about the process can impact the child's own faith in their schooling or in themselves. (Especially the sensitive ones). When ready and motivated, gifted children will catch up on any topic they are interested in, especially when taught in a way that suits them. (Often there is no stopping them!)

WHAT DOES IT LOOK LIKE?

In my work as a coach to parents of gifted and twice-exceptional children, many who are homeschooling, I have found deschooling in combination with unschooling to be effective and essential to getting back on track to learning. More often than not, certain topics continue to be a struggle until deschooling has fully occurred. While no two deschoolers are going to look alike, here is a timeline of Dennis's progression through deschooling math. Math is a subject that is often lost to creatively gifted children.

1ST GRADE: He is doing Montessori math and enjoys memorizing simple math multiplication and division problems, sometimes asking his mom to quiz him while they are driving. (Montessori school is not working for him for other reasons, however. While he enjoys doing math in his head, he does not like writing numbers down.)

2ND GRADE: He is back in the traditional school where he went to kindergarten. He dislikes math worksheets and asks why he has to do the same problems over and over. Math homework eventually becomes a shouting match nightly with his father. By the end of second grade, his mom has pulled him out of school to homeschool him for various reasons.

3RD GRADE: His mother homeschools him and learns that most curricula she tries out for him (and tutors she obtains), work for about a day before he loses interest. He has success going beyond grade level in fun ways in some other topics, but she can only find a "spark" for his love of math when YouTubing things that he brings up such as "infinity" and something called "Gold's number." At my suggestion, she uses this year to address some neurological issues and only has him learn what is interesting to him. This year is also about connecting with the gifted homeschooling community.

4TH GRADE: By fourth grade, she puts him in a microschool that understands school trauma and deeply understands the deschooling process. Dennis is still resistant to math, and they know to back off. The teachers talk about math concepts in terms of other topics, in non-intrusive ways. His first math "spark" is as follows: One obsession he has this year is flying. As part of this, he wants to figure out how fast he has to run in order to make a non-motorized flight suit take off. In order to measure how fast he is running, one of his teachers teaches him how to calculate his running in miles per hour. He comes home and is excited to show his dad how to figure that out. He tells his dad how to write the formula down. He remains resistant to doing the math on paper and writing it down formally with a math tutor.

5TH GRADE: In fifth grade, his interests are politics, economics, and government. For most of the year, his math tutor creates new problems related to these subjects such as figuring out the GDP of a country. Dennis is only able to stay engaged as long as there is a real-world relationship to why he is doing math, and when it is related to one of his areas of interest.

6TH GRADE: This year, another teacher, (the one who helped him calculate his running in miles per hour back in fourth grade), intuitively guesses that Dennis is ready for some formal math: for writing down equations and doing more basic math on paper, without needing a real-world problem each time. Dennis is now doing math equations and is excited and surprised at his own ability to do them. Because of the strong relationship he has with this teacher and his teacher's impeccable timing, this approach works.

7TH GRADE: He continues to have a great relationship with his math tutor, who is able to go at lightning speed for the kids who are ready to excel. By the end of the school year, Dennis is asking for additional math tutoring so that he can get ahead.

8TH GRADE: He is now at a different school, is taking his first group math class, and is requesting additional math tutoring in his free time. Dennis's mother reports that if you had told her when he was in third grade that he would be *asking* for extra math tutoring by 7th grade, (or any math at all, ever), she would not have believed you.

Is he looking like a typical eighth grader now? Not by a longshot. This was never the goal. This is perhaps the hardest part for parents of exceptional children to accept, and what I help parents to understand in my parent groups and my practice. He still has challenges that don't look like other eighth graders', such as spelling and writing, but he doesn't let them get in the way of his interests and classes. His friends have various challenges and areas they excel in, and this contributes to his ability to judge himself less by comparison. His teachers continue to create a culture of understanding for him where the students' abilities and disabilities are discussed openly and with respect. I see this in the gifted homeschooling culture as well. Not only does it help children and parents to understand weaknesses, it surprisingly opens doors to accepting gifts as well. This duality is difficult for many to comprehend, but these children understand it on a deep level when it is nurtured in them. (It's harder for the adults!)

Parents need to "deschool" as well. And it is harder for some than others. Dennis's father, who is an academic and values math and traditional education in general, tells me that it was like jumping into the void for him, and very anxiety inducing. It required a big, uncomfortable change in him, which included letting go of expectations of what he had assumed Dennis's education would look like and questioning what is really important for a child to learn. He had to deal with a lot of his own worry and fear about his son's future.

Contrary to how he was beginning to perceive himself in second grade, Dennis holds his head high because of this change in perspective that deschooling allowed him to find in himself again. He uses what is at his disposal to accomplish what he wants. He has friends who he writes articles and screenplays with. He hunts and pecks and doesn't mind that his spelling is off (for now). He uses technology to solve some of his problems – things that his parents could never have known would be available when he was younger, such as sharing a document with a classmate in real time while both are in their own homes. (Like online gaming, but in document form). His favorite class is history, a topic that his mother kept alive while he was deschooling. What is important is that he can accomplish what he wants. When the time is right, he may ask for more help. Or not. And that's ok.

I know that many families need to work within the traditional school's paradigm. In this case, I would use the information learned from gifted homeschoolers and alternative schoolers to inform how you frame your child's struggles and how to solve them. There is a lot that can be done outside of school. The most important thing you can do as a parent is to have faith in your child.

Deschooling is about teachers and parents being able to see the whole child and having faith in their abilities and their desire to learn, which includes understanding when to back off, when to drop seeds of thought, and when to allow the child to rise to a challenge. The overall goal is for the child to internalize this faith in their desire to learn and create that has been lost or injured. A faith that will last them a lifetime.

Why Intrinsic Motivation is Essential to Educating Our Exceptional Learners

Exceptional children who struggle in school, whether it is academically or socially, often look like they do not want to learn. Adults are often confused until they understand how much a child's intrinsic drive to learn is key to their success, both academically and socially.

While there can be so many reasons why a certain educational model doesn't suit a child, following the child's intrinsic motivation to learn with skill, integrity and most importantly, fun, seems to lead us to the solutions needed.

Just as most 2e/gifted kids will not eat something they do not choose (no matter how hard you bribe them!), many of us have found that they do not learn well if they cannot choose what, how, and when. They resist learning if it feels forced on them. This knowledge is often missing among those who subscribe to traditional schooling methods, and it is the reason that so many children are unhappy and failing in school.

Our strong-willed children have a built-in protective mechanism that prevents them from willingly accepting learning methods and topics that are an inappropriate fit for them. This often leads to behavior problems when they refuse to turn in homework, sit still, or do rote exercises.

Strong-willed or not, imposing inappropriate learning methods can result in a child with low self-esteem, severed relationships, depression, anger, and anxiety. They can look like they don't care about learning anymore, even the subjects they once loved. For some students, this internal backlash doesn't reveal itself until they are an adult. Some parents of 2e/gifted students find this to be true for themselves in hindsight as they learn about their own children.

Heartfelt and sincere relationships are important. It takes an empathic teacher who can meet them where they are, especially when learning doesn't follow the traditional trajectory. It also takes understanding parents to acknowledge that their child needs something different than the current learning environment. Once the adults in a 2e/gifted child's life fully understand this, there is less nagging, anger, depression, anxiety, and more learning, ease, freedom, (for the parents and teachers too), eventually allowing children to re-experience achievements.

For many of us new to gifted homeschooling and unschooling, educating a 2e/gifted child can take some time and a lot of trial by error. It's often a rite of passage in the gifted homeschooling world, that the parent doing the homeschooling tries to recreate traditional school for the first year, until they finally understand how their child learns and what they need: to follow their child's lead through discovering how they are intrinsically motivated and supporting those efforts. Parents of gifted homeschoolers often report a huge relief once they understand what learning looks like for *their* child, and find ways to ***allow*** the learning to happen.

This acceptance is a huge challenge for parents. As the father of an exceptional middle schooler said:

It requires a lot of patience and faith. Parents often have conflicting emotions that make accepting their child's needs very difficult. On the one hand, we can feel pride and excitement at our child's precocious understanding and achievements. Simultaneously it can be excruciatingly painful to patiently wait for him to hit traditional developmental milestones on his own terms,–which can sometimes take months or years longer than is typical. And to confuse matters further, some children sometimes show up right in the middle of the bell curve and the parents question the accuracy of their perceptions and intuitions regarding their child's needs.

Many child-led learning methods, such as microschools and gifted homeschooling, can have high withdrawal rates, as parents have a hard time trusting this unusual process. Families try to return to traditional schooling, only to be reminded that it doesn't work. I suspect this is largely in part due to a misunderstanding by the parents about what the child needs in order to learn. A huge misconception is that an alternative school, or homeschooling, is going to prepare the child to return to being more traditionally educated.

The "coursework" needed for real learning to occur may not even look like learning to the more traditionally-minded adult.

2e/gifted children often reach developmental milestones at uncommon ages, while some may never reach typical milestones. Alternative curriculum focused on 2e/gifted learners will allow the child to find their own strengths and thrive in their unique way, which I believe is what we all ultimately want. Until a parent understands this, there will always be friction and difficulty, and worse, the child's progress is undermined. For most parents, it takes a big leap of faith until, over time, (sometimes years), they see a change in their child, especially if healing from school trauma needs to occur.

WHAT ABOUT SPECIAL NEEDS AND LEARNING DIFFERENCES?

After understanding and/or addressing any neurological issues, scaffolding can be used to address special learning needs. Scaffolding is a technique that sets into place supports that allow the child to learn, create, and progress from the level where they are.

In the traditional school setting, students need to wait until they have addressed weaknesses before they can progress.

The combination of working on the weaknesses while not being allowed to progress in areas of strength usually increases boredom and, even worse, stifles the real work the student is motivated to do.

Take a child who has difficulty writing, but who has a strong interest in storytelling or journalism. Scaffolding might be allowing this child to dictate a story in order to give them space to explore their talent as a "writer" while supporting their challenge of not being able to write with pen and paper. Scaffolding usually doesn't mean tutoring in things like reading, phonics, typing, drills, etc., like you would expect from a traditional teaching approach. Sometimes a 2e/gifted child is not motivated to learn to type or edit their grammar until way into high school when they realize they will not be taken seriously unless they do so and are therefore intrinsically motivated to learn. It will take a non-judgmental adult to understand that this was not laziness on anyone's part; the child simply wasn't ready and didn't see the point. Once a child is ready to learn, only then will any learning challenges become evident.

As a side note, but an important point, because 2e/gifted children's brains are wired differently and development is asynchronous, sometimes they may look like they have a challenge when really their brain isn't ready until a non-typically developmental age. Often, exceptional children pick up on things they are motivated to learn at lightning speed once they are ready.

This can also happen to the student interested in subjects such as engineering or music, where finding ways to engage without lower math or learning to read music may need to be an option, at least for a while and for some, always. For some who are more creative, translating the creative (science or art) to the linear (writing or even verbal), or vice versa, can be debilitating to have to do before they are ready. Seemingly paradoxically, the child who does not prefer to "write" may go on to become a writer, the child who refuses to do repetitive math may go on to become a mathematician, and the shy child may actually become a gifted performer given the appropriate scaffolding.

These intensely creative and intellectually driven children are just that: fueled by their passions. For them, their education starts here and is the springboard for more growth. Most of us who have trusted this internal drive know that work ethic, grit, overcoming fears, and academics will surface only if they are *allowed* to surface – coming from this place between them and their teacher, not from any amount of external force, but from a place of mutual love: love for the material, love for each other, and love for their natural desire and drive to learn and grow.

I believe by refusing to learn in a traditional way, our 2e/gifted children are leading the way in voicing something about the public school system that is not working for most students, (gifted, special needs, or not). The world is changing, and the gifts that our most resistant and quiet students have to offer may be the key to resolving many of today's problems. Is our education system ready to listen?

The Benefits of Free Play in Nature

Have you ever noticed how freely children play in nature? Nature provides soft edges, new things to explore, and free items to build with. There is plenty of room for inspiration and creativity.

I took this picture one day at the beach. This is a floating raft that boys and girls of different ages built out of driftwood and large ribbon kelp. The kids in this picture didn't all know each other, and various kids came and went throughout the day. Some pushed and some made repairs by replacing pieces of wood. They all learned quickly how many the raft could hold, and exactly where they needed to sit or stand on it, and communicated this to each other by talking or watching.

No adults were needed in either the conceptualizing or carrying out of this project, which involved experimenting with concepts in engineering, physics, social skills, and a lot more.

In fact, as I watched the various phases throughout the day, there never seemed to be a sense of ownership of the raft, or more accurately, all kids who came and went seemed to feel they had a right to it. I watched the two siblings who my son said started the project much earlier, and they seemed to come and go just like the others. The one time I witnessed a child unintentionally harming the raft, the others corrected him.

More and more, we are finding evidence that being in nature and being allowed to play more often and freely is beneficial for children. In fact, when children are allowed to use playgrounds with more vegetation and less concrete, they show more creative play, better concentration, and more inter-gender play than on playgrounds without a natural environment.

All children deserve this.

Additionally, play in nature can address sensory needs. One example is how the two children standing on the raft are working hard to balance their bodies. This addresses their proprioceptive needs. Any exercise that requires balance helps to restore a sense of equilibrium to all the senses, and if you have a sensory kid, all the better.

Learning by playing in nature is perfect, and I think, necessary for all children. The experiential and visual-spatial learners are in their element, and the ones who are more comfortable with the linear-sequential become more flexible and creative. For the nature-loving, highly sensitive kids, time in nature is essential.

As Ken Finch, a writer about children's relationship to nature, in his article, "Free Play: Improvisation in Life and Art," states:

There is an old Sanskrit word, Lila (Leela), which means play. Richer than our word, it means divine play, the play of creation and destruction and re-creation, the folding and unfolding of the cosmos. Lila, free and deep, is both delight and enjoyment of this moment, and the play of God. It also means love. Lila may be the simplest thing there is — spontaneous, childish, disarming. But as we grow and experience the complexities of life, it may also be the most difficult and hard-won achievement imaginable, and it's coming to fruition is a kind of homecoming to our true selves.

If you observe successful, happy adults, especially those who are in creative fields such as mathematics, music, and the arts, and yes, even business requires creativity, a common skill they have is this ability to be playful. Being playful in work contributes to an individual's abilities as well as their ability to collaborate and to improvise. Important skills to have. Additionally, in my experience with highly sensitive and creative adults and children, playfulness can help to address the perfectionism that can otherwise be stifling.

As you know, when we are in joy, we are more likely to learn. Nature often inspires joy and connection. Connection with each other, connection to nature, and connection to ourselves – our true nature. Adults relax. Kids play. This makes the perfect environment for self-led learning. And for being.

5 Traits of the Young Empath

1) She is highly sensitive to stimuli, including noise, smell, touch, emotions. No two highly sensitive children are alike. She may hear a whisper across a room, or see the colors of the stars in the sky when others cannot. One in every 5 children is thought to be highly sensitive. (While there is no number for how many highly sensitive children are empaths, it is common in gifted children.)

2) He absorbs other people's emotions. This is the child in the large family who seems to be the one to get sick, emotionally or physically, when something is "off" in the family. He knows when mommy is upset, sometimes even before she does. He may also seem to take home anxieties and feelings from others at school. He is sometimes very good at doing impressions of people, or will take on a friend's mannerisms if he has been around him frequently.

3) She needs alone time and time in nature. Not just for the fun of it, but in order to function well. If in a constantly stressful, negative environment, she may not appear empathic, and can even be acting out in distress. When in a nurturing, loving environment, the empath can soar.

4) Learning to cope in life as an empath is going to be different for him. If you are an empath, learning the skills for yourself will help you to help your child. At the same time, when there is more than one empath in a family, the dynamics can get interesting. Mindfulness techniques can be especially helpful. Heart-centered approaches work best.

5) She is finely tuned to the pain of others. She will feel the pain as her own and try to help, sometimes without being asked, or even being conscious about it. For example, she wants to help every homeless person she sees, and becomes distressed when she cannot. She will need help navigating how and where she wants to spend her energy so that she does not become disheartened and drained.

Empathy Always Wins

Samantha was surprised. Her son was typically a very caring and empathetic child. So when he told her that he wanted to blow up his school, she wasn't sure how to react. She asked what would happen to everyone in the school if it were to be blown up. He explained that the school would be empty and that only the building would be destroyed. Still, she was troubled.

In addition, he told her that he "didn't like" a girl in his first-grade classroom who had developmental delays. She did what she felt was logical and explained to him that this little girl had a learning disability and, thus, special needs. The more she explained about the disability of the girl in his class, the angrier and more resentful her son became. She was disturbed by his reaction.

This is when Samantha called me. She explained that while her son was not incapable of mean thoughts and actions, in the past, those were usually due to some perceived wrong or hurt that had been done to him or to others. He had a strong sense of justice and was usually a fiercely loyal friend. Even when he was a baby, if another baby cried, he would cry too. Both she and her husband highly valued their son's feeling of compassion. She admitted that she was beginning to see other behavior that concerned her as well. Was her son becoming mean?

Samantha described how her son had recently begun begging not to go to school, and when he did go, pleaded for her to help in the classroom and on the yard. Periodically, the principal or teachers would report his misbehavior at school – striking out at other children and running into off-limits areas. At first, she and her husband simply asked him to "behave."

More recently, Samantha had been spending time at school and observed that, in fact, it was her son that was being bullied. She heard one story from a girl in her son's class. Every boy in their class was invited to be in the "boys club" except her son. One boy pretended to invite him into the club, as long as he would meet at a certain area on the yard, intentionally planning it so that no one was there. Her son had waited at the spot all during recess until he realized he was being made fun of. At first, Samantha couldn't believe it. She didn't want to. Could his "misbehavior" be in retaliation for being bullied, left out, and misunderstood? She was confused and at wit's end. She wondered with me if all of this could be related.

It is sometimes necessary to tolerate our own difficult feelings in order to model empathy for our children. It was painful for Samantha to bear the possibility of what her son had been enduring. She eventually came to understand that her son had felt unprotected by the adults at school. Even more difficult for her was realizing how she hadn't been able to guard him against harm over the years.

As we talked at length and through the process, Samantha revealed that this little girl with disabilities in her son's classroom had an adult assigned to her at all times by the school district. I pointed out that perhaps it wasn't that he didn't like her disabilities, or who she was, but that he needed the kind of support she was getting. Could her son be *jealous* of her? It was as though a light bulb went off for Samantha. This girl got special attention and protection from the adults – both things that her son was not getting. His behavior was beginning to make sense.

Later, Samantha talked with her son and asked if he was jealous of this girl. She later reported that he'd nodded yes. "Why does she get an adult to protect her, and I don't?" he asked.

Samantha's heart sank. But she continued. "It would be nice to have an adult understand what's been happening for you at school, wouldn't it? I wonder if you wish that you had an adult assigned to protect you. I wonder if you wish you had more people on your side." To which her son, whose first response to strong emotion was more often anger lately, nodded and became tearful. They hugged. She gave him all the compassion she had in that hug.

Samantha worked with the school to address the bullying that was now clearly happening. She eventually had to change schools to find a better fit, but her son is now making friends and thriving. Samantha continues to strive to raise a good human being.

Open Letter to a "Gifted" Teen

Dear "gifted" teen,

I put the word gifted in quotes because… you may not like it. Most adults still don't fully agree on what it means. You don't like the word, and perhaps it doesn't resonate with how you see yourself. Or maybe it does. It doesn't matter.

What's important is that you know that we are all living in a time where young adults know so many things that the adults don't quite understand yet. Probably this includes your parents, and even your teachers.

Maybe your parents are stressed about your plans for college, and so you are too. Maybe none of this, in some way, makes any sense to you. Maybe all you want to do is skip class and drive around with friends and then come home and start a business that you have an idea for. Or learn more about a very specific topic such as microbiology or psychology…. Or whatever!

Please, know that you are not alone. I hear this from others as well. And even within these "others," I see so many different struggles. If I put you all into a room together, you may not recognize it right away, but after talking for a bit, you might recognize something similar or familiar. I can't put you in a room, but when you find someone who seems familiar, please feel free to mention something unusual that you struggle with. See if there is a glimmer of recognition. If not, move on. If so, talk about it. Laugh about it. Stay in touch if that feels right. Even if you come from very different worlds. Even if they are 80 and you are 16. Maybe they are a jock and you are a theater type.

We are living in a time when, just like those videos and pictures of animals who would be unlikely friends (like a deer and a dog), are hanging out together, so are we. We need to have faith in who we are, as weird or strange as that may seem, and it helps to connect with others like us. Sometimes they are not wearing a similar outfit.

Fight to do what you are interested in. If you like physics, and your school's physics class is boring, know that you still get to like physics. Watch YouTube videos about it until you find something better. Fight for a better school. If your parents have the resources, look for an alternative school that is a better fit, or for alternatives to school. Pass the high school exam and take college classes. Find a mentor and start your business now. Get a job and start saving money for your dream. Start putting into action a plan that goes with what is important to you. The adults won't fully understand, but they will love your initiative. We all get depressed. Especially in these times. But having a goal, even if it is to hang in there through high school so you can go to college and finally study what you want, can help lift the depression. Know that you are not alone. There are many others out there. I know. I've talked with them. They don't like the word "gifted" either. It doesn't matter. Maybe the word is more for the adults to understand. Keep moving toward what you believe in. Keep the faith in yourself and in the world.

Best,
Teresa
(mother, therapist, gifted coach, friend, human)

Boredom in Motherhood: The Good, the Bad, and the Ugly

It's surprising, isn't it, how there are times when boredom is good. It's something we need not just to tolerate, but embrace. It can be the gateway to something amazing — like when your child tells you she's bored and you sit with it, not trying to create something for her, and she comes up with a creative project, or an idea that she begins or even carries out to fruition. Or, you think a walk in the woods by yourself will be boring, you do it anyway, and you come alive with self-reflection, new ideas, and stillness.

The bad can be when you notice that your child is constantly bored. He complains that school is boring. She doesn't seem engaged with friends. A constantly bored child can become depressed or turn to things that are both exciting and harmful.

One of the most fascinating things that I've discovered about motherhood is that a mother can be completely overwhelmed, anxious, busy doing all the right things for her family and be bored. I find that to be a huge paradox, one that can lead to misunderstanding the *why* of her sometimes-hidden unhappiness.

A first step is recognizing boredom for what it is. When we're out-of-our-mind busy, we'd never think "Oh, I'm so busy, I'm bored." We'll attribute our feelings of dissatisfaction to stress, "too busy," and all the other emotions that we associate with too much to do and too much to handle.

Unpacking the bored feeling can be helpful. What's the feeling about? Is it lack of intellectual stimulation? Or perhaps it's a lack of certain kinds of connection – maybe sensual, maybe deeper friendships (the kind that needs more than a playdate conversation). Where was I before becoming a mother?

Boredom can become a huge negative for a parent, especially for the mother who's taking care of the day-to-day of making sure a family is in working order. Here's the bad recipe: You may be problem solving at every corner, dealing with intensities and sensitivities, helping your kids grow so they can one day be on their own. You're not getting enough downtime alone, not making connections outside of your family, or both. Mix that with some overwhelm and tediousness (dishes, homework, laundry, bill paying – what's tedious for some can be relaxing and enjoyable for others), add some fatigue with a touch of lack of sleep. Now stir a little self-talk and a pinch of self-judgment into the mix, such as, "I'm a failure as a mother and whatever else I hoped to be, (what *did* I hope to be?), while everyone else seems to be going off to Hawaii (or has a successful career, or has a great relationship with her significant other, or seems happier than me, or whatever)." You have a perfect mom's recipe for The Ugly.

Many of us escape. And let's face it, some escapes from constantly being there for the troops are healthy and necessary. Your escape might be shopping if you have the money, a drink from time to time, a little gossip, cooking or food, time alone, or time with friends — we all have something that is and, must be, our little escape. However, sometimes we might become a little dependent on a painkiller, or maybe indulge in too much wine at the end of the day, or the gossip, or maybe the need to fix everyone else's problems is becoming a bit obsessive. Is your escape filling another need? Only we can know when something isn't serving us anymore.

Just as we need to find healthy ways to help our kids out of boredom, we must also find our own way out.

There are a variety of ways: supporting ourselves through friendships; jobs; projects; maybe even medication until we get on our feet; body-centered practices such as yoga, or running; finding a vocation or hobby that feeds our soul. Remember the kids who can go from boredom to depression or activities that are exciting and harmful? Well, we moms may need to take stock to make sure that our escapes come in the form of life-affirming self-care.

Letting ourselves feel vulnerable enough to admit this to ourselves is our power. Only we can know what our special way out of The Ugly is, and only we can know when the time is right.

BIBLIOGRAPHY

Gray, Peter. *Free to Learn: Why Unleashing the Instinct to Play Will Make Our Children Happier, More Self-Reliant, and Better Students for Life.* AZ: Basic Books, 2013.

Hollingworth, Harry L. *Leta Stetter Hollingworth: A Biography.* Bolton, MA: Anker Publishing, 1990.

Louv, Richard. *Last Child in the Woods: Saving Our Children From Nature-Deficit Disorder.* Chapel Hill, NC: Algonquin Books of Chapel Hill, 2008.

Roeper, Annemarie. *The "I" of the Beholder: A Guided Journey to the Essence of a Child.* Scottsdale, AZ: Great Potential Press, 2007.

Silverman, Linda Kreger. *Upside-Down Brilliance: The Visual-Spatial Learner* . Denver, CO: DeLeon Publishing, 2002.

Webb, James T., Edward R. Amend, and Paul Beljan. *Misdiagnosis and Dual Diagnoses of Gifted Children and Adults: ADHD, Bipolar, OCD, Asperger's, Depression, and Other Disorders,* 2nd ed. Scottsdale, AZ: Great Potential Press, 2016.

ABOUT THE AUTHOR

Teresa Currivan, LMFT, is a licensed marriage and family therapist, parent coach, former school therapist, and founder of The Right Place Learning Center. She speaks about differently wired children to teachers, faculty, and parent groups, and has published extensively on this topic. Teresa is recognized for developing the Currivan Protocol™ used to assess, address, and accept symptoms and co-occurring conditions in differently wired children such as ADHD, dyslexia, Sensory Processing Disorder, autism, executive functioning challenges, school refusal, depression, and anxiety. She received her MA in Counseling Psychology using Drama Therapy from the California Institute of Integral Studies in San Francisco and completed post-graduate training at The Psychotherapy Institute in Berkeley, California. She lives with her husband and son in the San Francisco Bay Area.

Teresa can be reached at TheRightPlaceLearning.com for:
- assessment
- counseling
- support
- school placement
..... for children and families.

www.ingramcontent.com/pod-product-compliance
Lightning Source LLC
Chambersburg PA
CBHW072337300426
44109CB00042B/1657